EMPLOYEE INDUCTION

Alan Fowler has worked widely in both the private and public sectors, with personnel appointments in four industries and two local authorities. He is now a freelance consultant, a director of Personnel Publications Ltd, and a member of the editorial board of *People Management*, the bimonthly journal of the IPD. He writes widely on personnel issues, with regular articles in *People Management* and the *Local Government Chronicle*. His books include *Negotiation: Skills and strategies*; *Taking Charge: A guide to people management in today's public sector*; *Redundancy*; and two Training Extras on *The Disciplinary Interview* and *Negotiating, Persuading and Influencing*. All are published by the IPD.

EMPLOYEE INDUCTION

A Good Start

Third Edition

Alan Fowler

INSTITUTE OF PERSONNEL AND DEVELOPMENT

First published 1983
entitled 'Getting Off to a Good Start'
Second edition 1990
entitled 'A Good Start'
Third edition 1996

Typesetting by The Comp-Room, Aylesbury
Printed in Great Britain by
Short Run Press Ltd, Exeter, Devon

British Library Cataloguing in Publication Data

A catalogue record for this book is available from the British Library

ISBN 0-85292-645-6

The views expressed in this book are the author's own, and may not necessarily reflect those of the IPD.

**INSTITUTE OF PERSONNEL
AND DEVELOPMENT**

IPD House, Camp Road, London SW19 4UX
Tel: 0181 971 9000   Fax: 0181 263 3333
Registered office as above. Registered Charity No. 1038333
A company limited by guarantee. Registered in England No. 2931892

Contents

Introduction

When organisations invest in new equipment they usually spend a good deal of time and money ensuring that it is properly installed and that it is quickly brought up to the planned performance levels which justified its acquisition. Preventive maintenance systems are operated to avoid breakdowns. Detailed performance and cost records are kept of servicing, repairs and down-time.

This care and attention to new equipment is unhappily in stark contrast to the often haphazard manner by which new employees are inducted into their jobs. Inadequate training results in progress towards satisfactory work performance being slow and erratic. A failure to explain rules and regulations can lead to serious misunderstandings and conflicts with colleagues or supervisors. Some new employees become disillusioned and resign; others may be dismissed for incompetence when an effective process of induction might well have resulted in success. Either way, avoidable direct and hidden costs arise. High rates of labour turnover push up recruitment costs. Low-quality work, high error rates and unnecessarily lengthy learning periods raise unit costs.

The importance of operating effective induction systems cannot be overemphasised. New employees need to have realistic expectations of their jobs. They need to be helped to fit rapidly into the organisation and into the working group. They need to know clearly what is expected of them: the standards and style of the work they are to perform. They need to understand their organisation's rules and regulations. They must know who is at work, and who can make decisions about which issues. They should be helped to develop their aptitudes and talents. They need to feel that their employer has a respect for them as individuals, as potentially resourceful people rather than as a mechanistic resource.

The changing recruitment scene of the late 1990s adds particular emphasis to the need for effective induction. In response to an increasingly competitive and fast-moving environment and technological change, employers are having to widen the basis of their recruitment, and introduce more flexible types of working arrangements. Conventional induction programmes for young trainees will not meet the needs of more mature re-entrants to work after long career breaks, nor will work-based programmes for full-time recruits satisfy the requirements of new part-time, job-sharing or home-working employees. Many induction training schemes will, consequently, need extensive revision if they are to meet the less standardised employment characteristics of the next decade.

This book is about effective induction, and its purpose is to help all managers, whether in personnel or 'in the line', to achieve the highest possible success rate among new employees. Induction cannot be considered as a wholly separate function from other elements of personnel management. It has particular links with recruitment, selection and job training. It needs, too, to take account of some aspects of employment legislation. This book does not attempt to describe all these related matters in detail. Instead, it pulls together elements of these other functions which have particular relevance to the management of new employees. It then sets these in a framework of induction procedures which span the period from job applicants' first contact with their prospective employers until the time, many months after first starting work, when it is advisable to decide whether they have really made the grade.

Care and attention to induction will secure the same high levels of productivity and efficiency among new employees as planned installation and preventive maintenance can achieve for new machinery and equipment. The effort that is needed is undoubtedly worthwhile. The ultimate reward, apart from direct improvements in the organisation's efficiency and competitiveness, is that the contribution that competent and highly motivated employees can make increases as years go by – unlike equipment, which begins to deteriorate from the first day it operates.

1

The Early Leaver

Employees are far more likely to resign during their first few months of employment than at any subsequent time. This phenomenon of 'the early leaver' has always been a problem for personnel managers, who see a high level of labour stability as one important characteristic of an effective, well-motivated labour force.

It is a persistent and very marked phenomenon. Writing of the period of full employment in the 1960s, Winifred Marks (the author of the IPD's first text on induction)[1] commented that in such a period 'more people change jobs by choice than of necessity'. The inference was that early leaving was encouraged by full employment. Studies in the 1950s had shown that among factory workers the proportion of leavers with less than three months' service was quite commonly between 40 per cent and 50 per cent.[2]

Yet in the 1990s early leaving did not disappear with the incidence of high levels of unemployment. Jobs were harder to get and labour turnover fell. But of those employees who did leave, a large proportion were still those with very short service. A study by the Institute of Personnel and Development in 1995 showed that well over 20 per cent of leavers had less than one year's service.[3] The study confirmed similar previous studies which indicated that the proportion of early leavers was highest among unskilled, part-time employees, and lowest among full-time, skilled manual and white-collar staff. It seems also that the time taken by a new employee to size up the job, and to decide whether or not it is suitable or congenial is less for unskilled than for skilled workers, but that in the latter category a peak of leaving still occurs during an early part of the service.

There seems to be a link between high levels of labour turnover and a high proportion of early leavers. Very high turnover, for example 50 per cent on an annual basis, will usually be linked with very high proportions of leavers with very short service (40 per cent or more in the first three months). If general dissatisfaction with the work is widespread, then a higher proportion of employees than normal will decide to leave very soon after joining.

There are also indications that early leaving is reduced by an intensive initial training period. In a 1982 study the figures for police and firemen were:

Category	% of leavers with	
	under 3 months' service	under 12 months' service
Firemen	3.6	7.1
Police	2.6	11.3

Both groups had very low levels of annual turnover (around 6 per cent), and a low proportion of early leavers is, therefore, to be expected. The percentages shown in the table, however, are very low indeed. It seems probable that this is connected with the fact that in both groups the new recruit has an intensive and full-time period of initial training followed by further on-the-job training, particularly during the first year of service. In both cases, too, selection procedures are more extensive and systematic than in much of industry, so the proportion of misfits should be considerably reduced, In these effects of selection and training there are lessons which form a major theme of this book. The use of statistics in monitoring early leavers is described in chapter 10 on page 88.

Does early leaving matter?

It may be asked, though, whether a high proportion of short-service leavers really matters? Is it perhaps merely a normal and largely unavoidable process of readjustment by which employees ultimately find the jobs that suit them?

There are at least three reasons for avoiding such complacency. First, a high incidence of early leavers can be very expensive. Take, for example, an accountant on £24,000 p.a. who leaves after only three months, during which time he has been far from fully effective. Supervisory and other staff time has been taken up during his short service with monitoring and correcting his errors.

2

His value to the company has been only about a third of his salary and oncosts. He leaves on one month's notice, but it takes two months to recruit a replacement. During the month's gap, the company has to use an agency accountant – whose charges (as is normal agency practice) are considerably more than the job's basic salary. The costs of this episode might well amount to:

Costs of extra supervision and error correction	£2,000
Gap between three months' salary and oncosts, and value to the company	£6,000
Additional costs of temporary agency replacement	£1,500
Recruitment costs of permanent replacement (advertising and management time)	£4,000
Induction costs (training, supervision and learning time) for replacement new recruit	£3,000
TOTAL COST	**£16,500**

Less dramatic individual costs for employees on lower salaries can still amount to a significant cost across a whole workforce. For example, if labour turnover for a staff of 200 clerical employees is 18 per cent (36 employees), of whom 25 per cent (9 employees) leave before they are fully effective, the annual cost of early leaving, calculated on a similar basis to the previous example, would be about £75,000. Cutting these costs by reducing the incidence of premature departures is therefore a worthwhile management exercise.

There is a second reason for attempting such a reduction. Early leavers are often disillusioned and disgruntled. They tend to put all the blame on the employing organisation with which they have patently failed to identify. Perhaps a few may have the insight and courage to say 'I made a mistake', but the majority will tell their family and friends that it was a rotten company. They will say that they were misled about pay or prospects, or that the management was abrasive or unsympathetic. In short, they will damage the organisation's reputation as an employer. The more this occurs, the less easy it will be to find good-quality recruits, and the likely result will be a repetition of early leaving.

Finally, the damage that a sequence of short stays can do to an employee's own career chances and aspirations should not be overlooked. Personnel managers should have a concern for the well-being of individual employees, as well as for the interests of their companies. Employers with an early leaving problem are damaging not only their own efficiency: they are exacerbating the unemployment situation by contributing to the pool of job applicants whose employment histories damage their chances of getting interviews.

Dealing with failures

So far we have commented only on employees who resign. There are two other categories that should not be overlooked. First, there are those who are dismissed at a fairly early stage in their service. It is obviously wise to use the first few weeks or months of employment to weed out employees who fail to come up to standard but who do not take the initiative themselves by resigning. If such dismissals are frequent, however, it must raise serious doubts about the adequacy of selection and initial training, and will certainly do harm to the employer's reputation.

Secondly, there is the other side to this particular coin: employees who should have been dismissed during the early or probation period but, owing to a lack of an effective appraisal system, have been overlooked until some disaster befalls. Most personnel managers can quote cases of line managers seeking a dismissal on grounds of incapability a few days after the first two years of service have been completed – just outside the period during which a dismissed employee has no access to an industrial tribunal. Of course, dismissals are to be avoided if at all possible. Far better, through training and counselling, to rehabilitate. It would be idealistic, though, to claim that selection and training can be so infallible as to guarantee the total absence of the odd recruitment error and of the occasional 'wrong-un' among the new recruits. The effective use of the first few weeks or months of employment to check on suitability and capability, and to take whatever corrective action may be necessary (including dismissal) is an important aspect of the management of the new employee. If a formal system of probationary service is used, induction becomes even more significant. Formal confirmation of the satisfactory completion of probation sets a firmer seal on an employee's suitability than mere survival past the two-year time limit of unfair dismissal legislation. The principles, however, are the same.

The importance of induction

Induction, then, is about all the steps an employer can take to try to ensure that new recruits settle into their new jobs quickly, happily and effectively. It must include some aspects of pre-employment procedures, cover formal and informal training activities during the early part of an employee's service, consider the respective roles of line and personnel managers in the various procedures (particularly counselling and performance appraisal) and have regard to employment legislation when such issues as contracts of employment, formal probationary service and dismissals are dealt with.

It is necessary, too, to distinguish the similarities and differences in induction needs of different categories of employees, and of different sectors of industry, commerce and public employment.

It is also important to recognise that employees involved in internal transfers and promotions require help in settling into their new jobs, as do those returning to work after lengthy career breaks. Home-based workers and part-time employees are often omitted from formal induction programmes, but their needs for assistance in adjusting to new working circumstances can be considerable. Planned, systematic and thorough induction should not be limited to new entrants, full-time staff and office- or factory-based employees.

Subsequent chapters cover the various practical aspects of the subject. The underlying theme, which this first chapter has highlighted, is that a thorough, systematic and well-planned approach to induction carries dividends to the employer in helping to secure a competent, motivated workforce, and to the individual employee by contributing positively to career development.

References

1 MARKS W R, *Induction – acclimatizing people to work*, London, IPM, 1970 (out of print)

2 EDC COMMITTEE FOR FOOD MANUFACTURING, *A Study of Labour Turnover*, 1967
3 INSTITUTE OF PERSONNEL AND DEVELOPMENT, *Labour Turnover Study*, London, IPD, 1995

2

The Causes of Early Leaving

Before going into detail about various induction processes, it is useful to consider why employees often find the initial employment period a difficult one. There is no single explanation, and in any one case of employee failure (early resignation or dismissal) more than one factor may be involved. Consideration of the most common causes nevertheless helps to point the way for corrective or preventive action.

False expectations during recruitment

Perhaps the most elementary cause is when the job and conditions of service do not in practice match the expectations created during the recruitment process. A common and rudimentary mistake is for the recruiting manager to be overoptimistic about earnings. 'The basic rate's only £200 but there's a lot of overtime, and the bonus scheme can give you another third.' This sort of statement builds up an expectation of regular earnings of over £300 per week. If, in practice, overtime is sporadic, and only employees with considerable experience maintain a one-third bonus, actual earnings for the newcomer may be little more than £225 and disillusionment will soon set in.

Generalised and equally optimistic statements about promotion or training opportunities can also be damaging. An over-enthusiastic portrayal of 'prospects' may lure applicants into acceptances of job offers. They will not stay long if their workmates pour cold water on such statements, pointing to Tom, Dick and Harriet who have all been with the firm for years with no career progression whatsoever.

Similar misunderstandings may occur about the work itself. The recruiter may overemphasise the unusual (and hence very interesting) but only occasional features of the job. Reality may show that in most weeks the work is simply boring routine. A

7

related problem occurs when the newcomer finds great difficulty in determining just what the job is. A new customer service clerk may be told that the work involves dealing with customer complaints and requests made by letter or telephone, but is given no check-list of typical problems or the correct procedures for dealing with them. A customer telephones with a complaint about a delayed delivery. The new clerk, using initiative, chases the factory production superintendent, only to be reproved for bypassing the proper channel of the production planning office. Such lack of clarity about who can make what decisions is a frequent source of frustration for the new employee in administrative, supervisory and managerial work. Inadequate or contradictory information about how to obtain tools and materials and what to do if breakdowns occur is a similar worry to new manual workers. The whole situation is exacerbated if instructions appear to come from a variety of unpredictable sources. 'I just couldn't find out who expected me to do what!' or 'Nobody seemed to know what was happening' are typical comments made by early leavers who have experienced this kind of confusion.

A more direct problem arises if the new employee finds the work too difficult or if, in the view of the management, the new employee is incompetent. In the manual sector, the absence of aptitude tests for work requiring a high degree of dexterity or co-ordination may well result in selection failures becoming evident within the first few days. Inadequate numerative ability for an office job involving statistical manipulation may take longer to show itself. A lack of managerial capability in a very competent professional (engineer, accountant etc), promoted for the first time to a general managerial role, may not be evident for many months. It is in this type of situation that potential redeployment or dismissal may feature as much as resignation. If required work standards are inadequately defined, the employee may not be aware of any shortfall. Resignations are likely only when the employee develops a strong sense of personal inadequacy and is reluctant to seek help.

Fitting into the organisation

Another cause of early leaving occurs when the new employee finds the whole style or culture of the organisation uncongenial or even downright unpleasant. Culture is sometimes described in simple terms as 'the way we do things around here'. Whereas this is an inadequate description of the complex cultural interaction between an organisation's formal and informal values, beliefs, customs, systems and structure, it does explain comments often made by early leavers such as 'It wasn't my sort of company' or 'I didn't like the atmosphere.'

Sometimes these feelings of incompatibility between the individual and the organisation are triggered by, or are focused on, a single issue, such as the way people dress or the degree of formality or informality in the use of first names when talking to senior managers. For example, in 1995 a large group of civil servants had to transfer to a private company when their work was contracted out. A staff attitude survey[1] a few months later showed that whereas many staff were enjoying new ways of working, one cultural factor was causing a very negative reaction and contributing to staff turnover. This was the company's conventions about dress (inspired by US codes) which expected men to wear dark suits and white shirts, with less easily defined but still powerful expectations as to how women dressed. Reaction against this was eventually sufficiently strong to worry the company about its ability to retain its staff, and managers were consequently told to adopt a more flexible and relaxed approach to dress.

The cultural factor is probably worth greater consideration at the selection stage than during induction. An organisation's culture can be thought of as its personality, and if the new employee's personality is markedly different then even skilled induction may be insufficient to achieve the new recruit's adaptation. A cautious perfectionist is unlikely to settle happily into a free-ranging, buccaneering type of company, whereas the imaginative extrovert will rapidly become disillusioned with an organisation that places an emphasis on accurate detail and adherence to procedures.

Relations with managers

A more direct form of personality clash that results in early leaving occurs when the new employee falls foul of supervision or

9

management. The risk of this is greatest when the selection procedures do not involve the employee's immediate boss. Recruitment may have been handled by a senior manager or the
personnel department, not the supervisor to whom the employee
will report on a day-to-day basis. On the first day at work the
employee and supervisor meet for the first time – and may take
an instant dislike to each other, with inevitable consequences.

But the problem can also occur even when the two have met
during the selection process if the supervisor or manager then
behaves very differently in the workplace. The latter may have
been very friendly and courteous during selection, but behave in
a far more formal or autocratic manner at work. The new
employee who has been influenced in accepting an offer of
employment by liking the style of the manager is then unpleas-
antly surprised by this change of character and may leave if the
situation is sufficiently unpleasant.

Fitting into the work group

A less tangible cause of early leaving arises when the new
employee has difficulty in adjusting to, or being assimilated into,
the immediate working group. There is a mass of scientific evidence of the power and importance of group psychology.[2] The
informal face-to-face working group develops its own style, standards and ethos quite separately from any formal organisation
structure or standards set by the company. Individuals within the
group develop particular and different roles. There will be the
unofficial leader, the joker, the conciliator, the innovator, the
devil's advocate, and the kindly aunt or uncle. A well-established
group will have a strong sense of its own identity with a ten-
dency to treat outsiders with reserve, or possibly with good-
natured scorn.

Into a cohesive group of this kind new employees are then
injected ie imposed from outside, not chosen by the group itself.
What role are these newcomers to play? If they ignore the
group's style and standards and work strictly to the formal, man-
agerially defined system, the group may see them as a threat.
They may therefore be frozen out or, at worst, actively
obstructed.

Extreme situations of this kind are, however, less common than those in which the new employee merely feels a degree of incompatibility with the general attitude or style of the group. For example, the group's approach to work may be one of jovial cynicism towards all company pronouncements about the need for higher productivity, and this may conflict with the new employee's genuine desire to work hard and establish a good working reputation. Similarly, a group whose approach is to bend the rules to get results will make an uncongenial working environment for the overparticular administrator.

It may be very difficult to identify instances of incompatibility within groups. By their very nature, informal working groups lie outside the formal and known organisational systems and standards. Furthermore, employees who resign because of a generalised feeling that they are failing to fit in (a sense of being socially uncomfortable) are often reluctant or unable to explain this. They will give more obviously rational reasons for leaving: 'I don't like the work', 'I can get more money somewhere else', rather than try to articulate the very much more diffuse and complex reasons for their unhappiness at work.

Exit interviews

Identifying the real reasons for the failure of new employees to perform or fit in is thus not as simple as it may first appear. The reason given by the employee may not be the basic reason: there may be a multiplicity of influences on the final decision to leave. Knowing what these reasons are nevertheless lies at the basis of all corrective action. The design of an effective induction process should thus start with an analysis of leavers' attitudes and problems, obtained by the personnel manager interviewing all employees who resign. Exit interviews can be time-consuming and demand considerable skill if they are to reveal the underlying reasons for an unsatisfactory level of labour turnover. They may even be considered undesirable by some supervisors who see them as a threat (eg the personnel manager listening to ill-founded complaints by malcontents!). But no personnel manager who wishes to ensure that the induction process fully matches the needs of the organisation can afford to disregard this

11

very direct source of information about what causes employees to resign (see also pages 89 and 90).

References

1 Attitude survey of Inland Revenue staff transferred to EDS Ltd, conducted by Opinion Leader Research for Inland Revenue Staff Federation, 1995.
2 There is a great deal of literature about working groups going back at least to the famous Hawthorne studies of Elton Mayo in 1924–32 (See F J ROETHLISBERGER, *Management and the Worker*, Harvard University Press, 1939, and E H SCHEIN, *Organizational Psychology*, Englewood Cliffs, Prentice Hall, 1970).

A useful summary of this, and other studies, is given in chapter 2 of K J PRATT AND S G BENNETT, *Elements of Personnel Management*, Denby, Gee & Co Ltd, 1979.

A useful summary of group concepts and dynamics is given in chapter 5 of JANE WEIGHTMAN, *Managing Human Resources*, London, IPD, 1990.

3

Pre-employment Action

All new employees start work with some expectations about their new jobs. These ideas are gained during the recruitment process and their accuracy or inaccuracy can have a significant impact on labour turnover during the critical first few weeks of employment. Disillusionment, if reality proves less attractive than an over-rosy picture painted during recruitment, is a potent cause of early leaving. More positively, some preparation for assimilation into the new job can be achieved before the first day at work, and so expedite the later induction process.

The job advertisement

Impressions about an employer begin to form even on first reading a job advertisement. Is the style formal or informal? Which is given more emphasis: job content or job benefits? Even the visual impact of the advertisement has an influence. Is it drab and old-fashioned in layout and typeface, or does it come across as modern, attractive and imaginative? From an induction viewpoint, this image and reality should be reasonably coincident.

Consider one extreme type of job advertisement: those which suggest very high rewards but say little or nothing about the actual work. 'Do you want to earn £1,000 per week?' These are almost always for direct selling jobs on a self-employed basis. Turnover during the first few weeks in such work is so high that advertising has to be virtually continuous. Perhaps the companies concerned would do better if their advertisements stressed the independence of the self-employed worker and the need in this kind of work for dogged persistence, rather than dangling a lure of apparently easy money. Overoptimism about earnings in job advertisements is a recipe for serious disappointment and reaction from new recruits.

Disillusionment can also occur through differences in style or character between the job advertisement and the working environment. An overimaginative advertising agency or an enthusiastic but inexperienced personnel manager may persuade a company to jazz up its advertisements with bright and breezy images and phraseology. The advertisement for customer service clerks, for example, may carry a photograph of a young, smart, smiling office worker, slimline telephone tucked under the chin, sitting at a glass and steel desk, backed by impressive office foliage. Suppose, however, the reality is a very ordinary office with the usual motley collection of wooden furniture, old-fashioned telephones, and a mainly middle-aged workforce. There may well be a case for refurbishing the office, but it needs to be done before the recruitment campaign begins, not after several young recruits have resigned.

It is to be hoped, too, that those employers who emblazon all their advertisements with the proud claim 'We are an Equal Opportunity Employer' really live up to their word. To eradicate prejudice and covert discrimination throughout a large organisation requires much more effort than inserting a slogan in job advertisements.

Care is also needed when briefing employment agencies or selection and search consultants, if these are to be the channel for initial contacts with potential recruits. Agencies often produce their own summaries of job details provided by their clients and it is good practice to vet these for accuracy before the assignment gets under way. It is not unknown for an agency or consultant unwittingly to give applicants a wholly distorted picture of the job and the company – a potential source of disappointment or difficulty at a later stage. For senior appointments for which an executive search consultant has been retained, it is essential that the consultant visits the organisation and spends sufficient time there to determine not just the detailed requirements of the job, but also the general characteristics of the job's organisational setting. Effective consultants not only brief candidates thoroughly about the nature of the work and give factual details of the client's business, they 'describe the client's corporate culture and management style . . .'[1] Getting this information right is obviously of critical importance, and one way of checking the consultant's understanding is to ask him or her to talk through what they intend to tell potential candidates.

The selection interview

What occurs during selection interviews is of even more importance than the job advertisement. Here, for the first time, the potential new employee makes personal contact with the potential employer, and may see the actual workplace and meet his or her potential manager or supervisor. The opportunity arises (or should do) for the applicant to ask questions, as well as to be told about the organisation and the job.

In practice, the extremes of approach are very wide. A single interview may be conducted by a recruitment officer (not the potential supervisor) at a hotel, or in the offices of the local job-centre. Because of time pressures the interview may be very one-sided, with no opportunity for the applicant to ask questions. Little or no recruitment literature may be provided. Job offers may be made by letter and include little more than basic information about conditions of employment. With this type of recruitment procedure new employees on their first day at work will be almost as ignorant of what the job and the employing organisation are really like as when they first saw the job advertisement.

Particularly in the public and voluntary sectors, candidates may have to attend panel interviews, sometimes involving as many as 10 or more members. These sessions can seem very formal and intimidating, but may bear little relationship in style or culture to the realities of everyday working life. Often, too, candidates are very confused about the identity and role of each panel member and may thus be unclear as to whether or not they have met the manager they would be working for. It is also generally difficult or impossible in panel interviews for candidates to ask detailed questions about the job or working conditions. Unless the interview is supplemented by a far more informal discussion with the personnel manager, candidates can be left with a very inaccurate and incomplete picture of what they would experience if they accepted an offer of employment.

At the other extreme, candidates may be gathered together in a group before the selection procedure starts and given a talk about the organisation, possibly supplemented with a film. They will assemble on the work premises and will meet, in addition to the personnel manager, line managers and their own potential direct supervisors. Before or after the interviews and selection tests there will be a conducted visit around the establishment and the whole process may end with a session in which the candidates can ask questions of a panel of the selecting staff.

When a procedure of this kind has been followed, a start has been made towards a formal induction programme before the new employee actually starts work. Not only will all the key information have been provided about the job and conditions of employment, but by meeting their potential bosses and by seeing the work location, potential new employees should have gained a good general impression of what working at this particular organisation would be like. The only danger arises when this type of highly structured pre-induction becomes much better organised than the work processes themselves. If potential employees are looked after better during selection than when at work, some disappointment is inevitable.

A less formal but still thorough approach may be better suited to most circumstances. A typical programme for an individual applicant may be along these lines:

10.00 am: Initial interview with personnel manager

10.45 am: If applicant considered a 'possible', conducted to workshop or office to meet potential supervisor. Supervisor walks applicant round to show work location and type of work in progress, followed by interview in supervisor's office

11.45 am: Applicant returned to personnel manager, either for immediate offer to be made, or to be told when and how outcome of interview will be notified. This session also used for applicant to ask questions, and to be told more about conditions of employment.

Essential elements of this routine are the quick, informal walk-through of the workplace; and the opportunity for applicant and supervisor to size each other up. The first day at work will not carry the terrors of the unknown if this important ice-breaking has been achieved earlier and before the applicant is irrevocably committed to employment.

Pre-employment documentation

There are four types of document that should be considered in the pre-employment period: literature about the organisation, details of conditions of employment, job descriptions and instructions about the first day at work.

Company literature

This type of information should provide some general scene-setting about company organisation, size and functions, but should also begin to foster an interest and pride in being its employee. Some thought needs to be given to match the type of literature to the kind of employees to whom it is issued. New managerial staff will not take kindly to being given something that is too obviously an idiots' guide, while school-leavers starting in unskilled jobs are unlikely to be enthusiastic about a copy of last year's annual report and accounts. A copy of the latest house journal may help to provide an insight into the organisation's activities and style.

For pre-induction purposes all such literature has a somewhat limited value. New employees' overriding concern is with the details of their new jobs. An interest in the wider company scene develops on the foundation of integration within the particular workplace.

Conditions of employment

These documents are of great importance not only legally but also because the information they contain about earnings, pensions, holidays, hours of work and so on plays an important part in the applicant's decision to accept an offer of employment. To avoid later problems, and ensure that the potential employee has a thorough and accurate understanding of the terms of service, these documents need to be comprehensive, but also easy to understand. Although legislation permits 'written particulars of employment' to be issued to new employees at any time within their first two months of service, it is clearly advisable to issue these details with offers of employment. The most important legal point is not this two-month period but the list of information that the Employment Protection (Consolidation) Act 1978 (as amended by the Trade Union Reform and Employment

Rights Act 1993) requires to be set out in the written statement, or in related documents. This includes:

- the name of the employer
- the date of commencement of employment
- the date (if different) when the period of continuous employment began
- the scale or rate of pay, or how pay is calculated
- the intervals at which remuneration is paid
- terms and conditions relating to hours of work
- terms and conditions relating to holidays and holiday pay
- terms and conditions related to sickness absence and sick pay
- terms and conditions relating to pensions
- notice periods
- the job title or brief job description
- if the job is not permanent, its likely duration or the date it is expected to end
- the place or places of work
- a reference to any collective agreements that affect the terms and conditions
- disciplinary and grievance rules and procedures.

The formal contract of employment, or the standard schedule of terms and conditions, may have to be written in a fairly terse and legalistic style. For a number of important items no more may be said than, for example: 'Overtime is paid in accordance with the National Agreement for the industry's manual workers.' The formal information about pensions (a critically important employee benefit for many applicants) may use unexplained jargon such as 'reckonable service may exceed pensionable service but counts only towards qualifying periods'. An explanatory leaflet or booklet about all the important conditions of service, including pensions, written in an informal, easy-to-read style is of great assistance in ensuring that new employees do understand their entitlements. It should certainly include details of items covered by national agreements which are not set out in the formal documents. To protect the employer's legal position, the explanatory leaflet may need to include a statement to the effect that 'the purpose of this leaflet is solely to help employees understand the details of the company's conditions of employment and does not form part of the contract of employment.'

Job descriptions

Full job descriptions may also be issued with the formal contract documents. It is advisable for them not to form part of the actual contract as this may inhibit flexibility in deployment at a later stage, but as a guide to the nature of the work they are extremely useful. Any apparent differences between the formal contract and the job description should be explained. For example, the contract may specify only a very general form of appointment such as 'assistant administrator', and state that the employee may be required to work 'in such departments and locations as the company may from time to time require'. The job description, however, may be very specific and set out the duties for a particular post, say, 'sales offices administrative assistant'. This is the job in which the new employee is to start, but from which a transfer may be made at any time. To avoid later misunderstandings, it is essential that the new employee understands the difference between the first appointment and the wider contractual obligation to accept transfers to other work. Ambiguities must be eliminated from all pre-employment documentation. (See Chapter 5, page 31 for job descriptions as working documents once employment has begun.)

Starting instructions

Instructions given or sent to the new employee before employment starts bring the new employee to the door on his or her first day. They should be helpfully explicit about such basic details as where and when to report on the first day and what, if anything, to bring. The following check-list shows a number of points about which the new employee may worry if no information is provided:

Time: should this be the standard starting-time, or a little later to ensure that reception staff, supervisors etc are present when the new employee arrives?

Place: which entrance should be used? If reporting to a department, which location or room number?

Person to see: who is first going to see the new employee, or for whom should he or she ask?

19

Car parking: if the new employee is likely to travel to work by car, where should the car be parked?

Clothing: are there rules about clothing at work? Or will protective clothing be issued?

Tools: are employees expected to supply their own toolkits?

Documents: is a reminder necessary about bringing documents such as the P45, and a signed copy of the contract of employment?

Security: are any instructions necessary about security? Is it necessary to show the starting letter or a pass to the security staff?

Catering: would a brief reminder about the company's catering facilities be helpful?

Medical examination: does the new employee have to undergo a medical examination?

New employees are often worried that on arrival on their first day they may use the wrong entrance, or lose their way in complex office or factory premises. In a large organisation a sketch map showing the right entrance and the reporting location is of great help. They also want to know whom they are going to meet, and this should be preferably someone they have already met during the recruitment process. For some types of work they may worry, too, about wearing the right clothes; this is a point that may be touched on during recruitment, but it should be repeated in the starting instruction if the matter is at all important.

Conclusion

Pre-employment induction will have served its purpose if the new employee can look forward to the first day at work with some confidence. On going home at the end of the day, the new employee's family may ask: 'What was it like?' If pre-employment induction has been effective, the answer should be along the lines of 'It was good and very much what I expected.'

References

1 JONES S, *The Headhunting Business*, London, Macmillan, 1989. For

various aspects of recruitment and selection, see: J. COURTIS, *Interviews: Skills and strategies*, London, IPM, 1988; J. COURTIS, *Recruiting for Profit*, London, IPM, 1989; J. COURTIS, *Recruitment Advertising*, London, IPD, 1994.

The First Day at Work: Reception and Documentation

However well prepared the new starter may be, some trepidation about the first day in a new job will always remain. Although this may be more marked for the school-leaver who is entering paid employment for the first time, even senior managers starting in a new employment will, if they are honest, admit to first-day nerves. The importance of planned induction on the first day is therefore obvious, although there is also a risk of attempting too much in one day. A too intensive one-day programme of introductions to numerous members of staff, tours of the factory or office, and a series of talks about the organisation and about conditions of employment could well be more confusing and stressful than merely starting the actual job with little preparation.

It must be remembered that new employees on their first day will not be wholly relaxed, and will be primarily concerned with immediate practical matters such as locating their workplace, finding the lavatories and the canteen and meeting their immediate working colleagues. They will not be receptive to a great mass of new information, particularly if much of it has no immediate relevance to the overriding need to get through the first day without making some embarrassing mistake.

Initial reception

As noted on page 19, the letter confirming the appointment should ensure that the new employee gets to the right reception point at the right time. If all new starters have to report to a general reception desk, the receptionist should be provided with a list of those expected each day, with instructions about where they are to be directed. An informal welcoming word from the receptionist, showing that the employee is expected and making an initial personal contact, will get the day off to a good start.

The importance of this first contact can be emphasised by

looking at the effect of a badly organised introduction. Here, the new starter goes to a reception point, only to find it unmanned. After a worrying wait, a receptionist appears, takes the newcomer's name and, after looking puzzled, asks the starter to wait. The receptionist, possibly a general purpose security officer, then picks up the telephone and can be heard to say: 'I've got a Miss Jones here who says she's starting work in Accounts. What do you want me to do with her?' After some further telephone chat, the receptionist says to Miss Jones: 'You're in the wrong place; you should have gone to the staff entrance to the Admin block – it's down the stairs, turn right, across the yard, left by Goods Inwards, and through the green doors in the old building nearly opposite behind the car park.' Miss Jones will eventually arrive at her workplace late, flustered, in no state of mind to absorb detailed instructions about her job, and with a first impression of being a very small and not well-meshed cog in an impersonal and unfriendly organisational machine.

Not all organisations require starters to report to a general reception point. In some offices or factories, new employees go direct to their section manager's office. In large-scale retailing they will most probably report to the staff manager. In construction, the site labour officer or the general supervisor may be their first contact. In many organisations all new starters report on their first morning to the personnel office. Whatever the precise arrangements, the same check-list can be applied:

- Ensure that the person whom the starters first meet (ie the receptionist, secretary, or personnel assistant) knows of their pending arrival and what to do next.
- Set a reporting time, which will avoid the risk of the starter turning up before the reception or office staff arrive.
- Train reception staff in the need for friendly and efficient helpfulness towards new starters.
- If the new starter has to go on to another location immediately after reporting, provide a guide, unless the route to the other location is very straightforward.
- Avoid keeping the new starter waiting: steady, unhurried, guided activity is an excellent antidote to first-day nerves.

Documentation

Once past the initial reception point, one of the first formalities is to complete any necessary employment documentation. The new starter will be requested to hand over the P45 income tax form from the previous employer, or in its absence may need an explanation of the resultant emergency tax coding. There may also be a card or form of some kind to complete from an employment agency. The organisation itself may issue a variety of documents to new employees, some of which may require signatures for their receipt. These may include:

- employee handbook
- identity card or security pass
- canteen pass or tokens
- clock card or time-clock key
- locker keys
- car park permit
- authorisation to draw protective clothing or tools from stores
- membership card for social club
- documentation for company car
- company rulebook (including details of disciplinary and grievance procedures)
- safety rules and safety literature.

It may also be necessary for the employee to provide some information for personnel records, additional to that obtained during the selection process. This might include:

- details of next of kin, with telephone contact during working hours
- name and address of GP, if required for medical check
- driving licence and car insurance certificate (certificate may require endorsement for business use)
- first aid certificate, if relevant
- birth certificate – for pension or life insurance records
- passport or work permit, if not a UK citizen
- details of previous pension arrangements for possible transfer purposes.

Many organisations now require employees to carry an identity card or badge that includes a passport-type photograph. Recruits should be told in advance if they need to supply a photograph, or whether one will be taken on their first day.

These check-lists illustrate one possible danger – that of over-burdening the starter with too much initial information and with too many documents. If some of the items listed are not essential on the first day there is much to be said for issuing only the most necessary at that time and dealing with the others over the following few days.

---------------------------------- 5 ----------------------------------

The First Day at Work:
Introduction to the Workplace

Unless starters spend their first day attending some form of training course (discussed in the next chapter), the first day will require a planned introduction to the actual workplace.

Starters will have three immediate concerns:

● What is the geographical layout? What routes should be taken to and from the main entrance? Where are the time clocks (if any)? Where are the lavatories? Where is the canteen?
● Who's who? Who and where is the immediate supervisor, the section manager, and other important staff? Who are the immediate working colleagues? Who allocates the work? Who is going to explain what?
● What work is actually going to be done during the first day?

For induction purposes, the most important question here is: who is going to explain what? The answer is most unlikely to be just one person. No supervisor is likely to have sufficient time to explain all the many practical details involved, though all supervisors should accept a heavy personal involvement in the induction of newcomers. A useful approach may therefore involve five people: the personnel professional, the supervisor, the senior 'manager, a 'starter's friend' and a job tutor.

The personnel officer

It is helpful for all the administrative matters involved in initial documentation to be dealt with before new employees go to their actual places of work. They will have brought documents with them, such as the P45 tax form, and will want to hand these in as soon as possible after they arrive. They may also need to be issued with other documents such as security or car park passes or canteen vouchers. All these preliminary matters can usefully be handled by the personnel department as the first activity in the first day's induction process.

If the first contact is therefore with the personnel manager or other personnel professional, this also provides an opportunity to set the scene for subsequent induction activities and to establish an immediate personal contact between the organisation and the new employee. This first contact can do much to put starters at ease and show them that they are being welcomed as individuals. The personnel officer who has the responsibility for meeting new employees on their first day should also take them to their workplace and introduce them to their manager or supervisor.

The supervisor

It is essential that the new employee is met at the workplace by his or her supervisor. The same supervisor will preferably have taken part in the final selection process, so that this should not be a meeting of strangers. In any event the person to receive and welcome the newcomer to the department or section should be the supervisor or manager to whom the new employee will report on a day-to-day basis.

The quality of the personal relationship between supervisors and their employees is extremely important, and this first meeting can set the tone for the future. It is the supervisor's first opportunity to establish a positive rapport with his or her employees, and a friendly, helpful – but firm and positive – approach to this first meeting will do much to establish the supervisor's later influence. The induction of new employees should form part of any supervisor's training, and it is a responsibility that supervisors must be encouraged and be expected to take seriously.

The supervisor, then, should meet the new employee and explain some of the initial dos and don'ts. Some aspects of induction may be delegated to other staff, but information about timekeeping and any important safety regulations should come directly from the supervisor. Only by such direct explanation will the importance of the principal rules and regulations affecting everyday working life be sufficiently emphasised. This may also be the first opportunity to explain the organisation's core values, such as quality and customer service.

27

In some sectors other essential points may require similar personal emphasis by the supervisor, such as:

- in manufacturing – the key rules about quality standards, the reporting of breakages or tool losses
- in retailing – rules about staff purchases, customer complaints and stores security
- in offices – any standard drills for answering external telephone calls, or for the style of official letters
- in some local government jobs – key points about staff conduct relative to elected members, the public and the press, and restrictions on political activity.

The senior manager

Either on the first day, or as soon as possible thereafter, the supervisor should introduce the new starter to the appropriate senior manager who has overall responsibility for the department or location. The size and type of the organisation will determine who this should be. Obviously, in a large multiplant company the managing director cannot meet every new shopfloor or office worker. But senior managers should make every effort to meet as many of their employees as possible.

It is a particular feature of Japanese management, including Japanese plants in the UK, that the factory manager meets each new starter and so establishes a personal contact at the earliest stage of employment. UK managers are often criticised by their workforce for being too remote. A routine in which the supervisors introduce their new workers to their senior managers can go some way to establishing better working relationships. The investment of a little managerial time in showing an interest in employees as individuals will be amply repaid by the positive and co-operative attitudes it can help to promote.

The starter's friend

The supervisor should also introduce the new employee to his or her immediate work group and, if there is one, to the group's chargehand or section senior.

One of this group should be selected to act as the starter's initial guide, primarily to ensure a knowledge of the geography and perhaps to provide practical tips about the more informal dos and don'ts of working life. It is helpful for this 'starter's friend' to be the same sex and of a similar age and background to the new employee. A middle-aged woman is unlikely to feel at home being shown round by a teenage lad or *vice versa*, particularly as washrooms and lavatories need to be included in the itinerary.

There is also much to be said for these initial guides to have fairly short service. As relative newcomers, they are likely to remember all the little points which were a potential source of worry to them when they started work, and so help new starters learn the ropes rapidly.

They should, of course, be selected for this work in advance of starters' arriving, and given instruction as to what is needed. It is helpful to issue them with a short check-list of points to be covered in the first day. It is likely to include the following:

● location of entrances and exits and time clocks
● routes to and from the canteen, lavatories, car park, rest room, first-aid room, supervisor's/manager's/personnel department's offices
● location and any particular procedures for cloakrooms, changing rooms, tool or clothing stores
● location of vending machines and purchasing system (eg tokens)
● canteen procedures (eg cash, tokens, authorisation cards etc). Tips about informal canteen customs, ie who usually sits where and when, will also prevent unnecessary embarrassment.

The type of employee needed as a starter's friend is one who will be helpful but not overbearing, good at explanation, sufficiently relaxed to be relied on to chat about informal aspects of the job, and reliable in the sense of covering the necessary ground and not passing on bad working customs. It is also cost-effective to use a more junior employee in this role rather than to take up the time of higher-paid supervisory staff.

The job tutor

The full process of learning the new job may take many weeks. In much work this is aided by some form of off-the-job instruction. For some activities an initial full-time training period in a training section or a separate training centre may be essential (see Chapters 6 and 7). Here, we are considering only the first working day for jobs where the new starter is not required to follow a formal job training programme.

The right person to act as guide at this time may not be the right employee to teach the new employee the actual work involved in the job. For this, an experienced employee is essential, one who has been trained in the skills of job instruction. It is not unusual for this task to be allocated to the chargehand or section head of the working unit. Where this is not so, it is still a function that needs to be recognised as being of critical importance, and for which preparation is essential. Even if supervisors have insufficient time to train new starters personally, it is essential that they monitor the quality of the job training carried out in their sections. However busy they are with other duties, they should certainly take time to check the progress of every new starter at frequent intervals and to reinforce key elements of job training by personal instruction.

There are two complementary principles for the trainer (supervisor or experienced worker) to bear in mind for this first day:

- Do not overload the new employee with too much information. For the first day, the simple basics of the job are adequate. Have a training programme that takes in the wider or more complex elements of the job on a phased basis over subsequent days.
- Do keep the new employee busy. There is little worse for an ill-at-ease newcomer than having nothing to do. The new employee can be made to feel embarrassingly isolated and conspicuous if left sitting at an empty desk or standing at an idle machine while everything around is a hive of activity.

The emphasis should be on an explanation and demonstration of a few of the basic work tasks, and the allocation of sufficient appropriate work to enable the starter to do something useful without too much obvious supervision. Trying to cope with a new job under direct and continuous observation is particularly trying. What is needed is a fairly frequent check on progress, without breathing down the newcomer's neck.

Documents about the job

Three types of document may assist the initial job learning process: job descriptions, equipment manuals and job or procedure schedules.

Job descriptions

These may have been included in the documentation issued before starting work. At this stage they may have seemed rather formal or abstract. On the first day they gain significance and should be used by the supervisor or section head as an aid to job instruction. They may, for example, be used as a check-list, showing the starter which elements of the whole job have been covered in the first day, and which have been deferred until later in the learning process. It is often important to emphasise to new starters that the job description is a general guide and not a wholly comprehensive or restrictive schedule and also that other duties generally appropriate to the job may occur from time to time.

Many organisations include as a final item in the job description, after all the specific functions have been described, a statement that the job-holder will also be expected to undertake 'such other duties as the management may reasonably require'. If this is not explained some new employees may fear that it is a catch-all phrase which enables their managers to require them to do almost anything, however remote from their normal work. This is not the case, because it does no more than confirm a common law principle that employees can be expected to undertake any duties broadly and reasonably consistent with their expertise, status and general type of work. Thus it would probably not be unreasonable to require a secretary to oversee the loan of books from an office library (even if this was not in the original job description), but it would almost certainly be unreasonable to add office-cleaning duties.

The precise situation in any organisation depends as much on established custom and practice as on the words used in a job description, so it is not possible to give wholly definitive examples. The important point from an induction viewpoint is that the possibility of being asked to undertake duties not in the job description should be explained.

It is also very important to explain if any requirement may arise for a transfer to another department or location. As outlined in Chapter 3, page 19, job descriptions sometimes include some form of mobility clause, and it may be very worrying to new employees to think that at any time they might be required to relocate. An early explanation of the probability of this occurring, what would be involved and what assistance the organisation then provides will reduce new employees' concern.

Equipment manuals

These should always be available for computer terminals, word processors, photocopiers and other similar equipment. It is usually necessary to demonstrate the operation of such machines to new starters who are unfamiliar with the particular models in use, but instruction manuals should also be issued. Many word processor operators, for example, prefer to learn the operation of new software by teaching themselves from the equipment manual, rather than by having to rely on their supervisor's or colleagues' tuition. Some manuals, however, are very poorly written for teaching purposes, and may need supplementing or replacing with a clearer set of operating instructions written by the organisation's own training staff. Office or reception staff might also be provided with their company's general sales literature. This will help to ensure that they project the image of a well-informed workforce and will develop their interest in the ideals and objectives of the organisation for which they work.

Many software packages for word-processing and other computer applications include a self-teaching program for the new user. Some of these are excellently written and can be relied on as the main instruction method. Others, however, are less satisfactory and can cause the new employee (or the existing employee who has to learn a new job or work system) considerable frustration. These programs should also be tested for their 'teachability' – preferably by asking a wholly inexperienced person to try to follow them. Even with the best programs, and always with the less satisfactory, it is as well to designate an experienced user to be available to help the new employee who experiences difficulties. The problem with all computer programs is that one very minor error in their operation usually brings the whole process to a stop. Misreading an instruction (eg assuming that 'Press Alt+F1' means that the two keys are pressed one after the other instead of together) prevents any further progress. The new employee needs quickly to be able to turn to an experienced user and say 'I'm stuck: what have I done wrong?'

Procedure schedules

Schedules of working procedures should be used more widely. Too often, new employees have to learn for themselves how particular elements of the work ought to be done, or what procedures to follow to undertake particular job functions. Job descriptions tend to emphasise responsibilities, eg 'responsible for daily sorting and distribution of internal mail', but do not say how these responsibilities are actually discharged. The following example shows how a simple procedure schedule can be much more helpful to the newcomer:

Daily procedure for internal mail

1 Between 9.00 am and 9.30 am each morning, collect mail from pigeon hole E in room 218.
2 Open all mail, except sealed envelopes marked 'personal' or 'confidential'.
3 Stamp all opened mail and all unopened private or confidential envelopes with date and time stamp.
4 Sort mail into six trays (marked with section titles), using internal phone directory to identify relevant sections where only employees' names are given.
5 Refer any queries to administrative manager in room 103.
6 Take sorted mail to the six section heads (room numbers shown on trays); should be completed by 10.15 am.

Obviously, different procedure schedules will apply to different types of work, but the principle of setting out a step-by-step instruction for all the main working tasks can be applied to almost all jobs. For a simple factory task, for example, a schedule might be along these lines:

Packing procedure

1 Take packing box from pallet at left of machine and place on left side of packing bench.
2 Take two polystyrene packing pieces from bin A and fit over ends of completed unit.
3 Place packed unit into box, top side up.
4 Lay instruction leaflet and guarantee card on top of unit.
5 Seal box with tape from dispenser on right of bench, as shown in diagram on wall.
6 Place sealed box on pallet at right of bench.

At more senior levels, the documentation of procedures for such matters as obtaining staff, placing purchasing orders, reporting production results or reporting accidents or stock losses aids the rapid adaptation of new staff and eases the burden of training or explanation by existing supervisors and managers.

The Welcome Pack

Some organisations incorporate all the documentation for new employees in a specially designed Welcome Pack. This may be a looseleaf file or folder into which all the different documents referred to in this chapter can be inserted. But it also has a short opening page or section addressed to the new employees, often in the form of a personal message from the chief executive. It may also include details of the names, jobs and locations (and perhaps photographs) of all the people the new recruit will be introduced to during the first few days: the supervisor, senior manager, health and safety representative, shop steward, and starter's friend. Starters should be encouraged to keep the pack as a reference source to be used over a period of many months, rather than as a document to be read in full, and immediately, and then discarded.

The trade union contact

Apart from the section supervisor and working colleagues, there may be one other personal introduction to be made on this first day: that to the section or departmental shop steward. This will depend on the procedures agreed with the trade unions, and in some organisations may not apply at all. In others, unions may be supplied with names and work locations of new starters and any personal follow-up is left to the shop stewards. Where employees are highly unionised a personal introduction by the section supervisor may, however, be desirable. Even if this is not considered necessary, new employees should certainly be told if they are likely to be approached by the stewards, and given an indication of the organisation's attitude to union membership. The form of these explanations might be:

A Mr Brown may come to see you. He's the shop steward for the T&GWU. It is entirely up to you whether you join or not. The company considers that it is something about which employees should make up their own minds without any pressure either way.

Or:

Mr Brown, our T&GWU shop steward will be seeing you soon. We don't run a closed shop, but by and large we think it is a good thing for most people to join unless they have very strong views against.

It is as well, too, to have an understanding with the trade unions about the nature of their approach to new employees, particularly if several unions are competing for membership. It is undesirable in such situations for one particular steward, who happens to get in first, to give a new employee the impression that only that union exists, if within a short period the employee is going to be approached by one or two other recognised unions. New employees should have the situation explained to them.

Although the UK has opted out of the provisions of the European Social Chapter, this, and other European legislation, is encouraging the introduction of works councils – or at least the election of employee representatives, whether or not these are trade union members. The first day is generally too soon to explain everything about the role of a works council, but if the new starter's section has an employee representative, he or she should be among those to whom the starter is introduced.

6

The Induction Course: Attendance and Scheduling

Many employers, particularly those with large numbers of employees and, consequently, significant numbers of recruits, find it helpful to deal with induction on a more formal basis than has been discussed in the last two chapters. In short, they prefer to run induction courses.

Purpose of an induction course

There are several reasons for the above-mentioned preference:

- Dealing with recruits in groups saves considerable time that would otherwise be spent by personnel managers and supervisors going over the same ground with each individual starter.
- An efficiently planned training course will ensure that all necessary information is relayed consistently to all new starters. It will guard against the omissions that can so easily arise if induction is left to *ad hoc* action by busy supervisors.
- Within an effectively designed induction course a full range of techniques can be used to assist in the assimilation of information: videos and other visual aids, discussions, 'chalk and talk' lectures, planned visits, and working projects. Few of these techniques can be used during informal induction.

At the same time, there are some potential dangers in relying wholly or mainly on formally organised courses. In particular:

- An induction course may be far more organised than 'real life'. It may be highly structured not only in its content but in terms of its hour-to-hour organisation. Trainees may, in effect, be so spoon-fed on the course that the eventual transfer to work may consitute the very kind of culture shock which induction is designed to prevent.

- Trainees may suffer from a surfeit of information if all induction is packed into one training course at the beginning of employment.
- Any induction course has to include a fair volume of information, much of it detailed. Furthermore, some of this information is likely to be fairly remote from day-to-day working experience. For example, an explanation of company structure or of a complex pension scheme has little immediate relevance to a young starter in a fairly basic job.
- If only personnel and training staff are involved in running induction courses, starters are left unassisted on one most important element in their induction: their absorption into the social fabric of the organisation. Getting to know line managers and supervisors and adjusting to their style, 'tuning in' to the ethos and attitudes of working groups – these are aspects of induction that cannot be dealt with by personnel and training staff alone within the confines of a formal training course.

Despite these potential risks, any organisation with a sufficient inflow of new recruits to provide satisfactory training groups is likely to find that the benefits of an induction course far outweigh any disadvantages.

In planning such a course a number of factors need to be considered:

- Should the course be designed for a single category of staff, or draw together new starters from a variety of occupations and levels?
- How should it be structured and scheduled? Possibilities include a half or whole day on the first day at work; a much longer initial period in which induction training merges into initial job training (perhaps in a training centre); or a course covering several days but spread over a number of weeks on a day-release basis.
- What training techniques are to be used – videos, talks, discussions, visits?
- How much of the whole process of induction should be included in the course, and how much left for managers and supervisors to deal with at the workplace?

Choosing the course attenders

If the organisation employs large numbers of staff within one particular category (eg retail shop assistants in a large department store; semi-skilled, general purpose factory workers in a large assembly plant) the induction course can be designed especially for this group. It can concentrate on the very specific details of one particular type of work, and may then be linked with initial job training.

But many organisations are multifunctional, and even the simpler type of company will have a sprinkling of new starters in types of work other than the main occupation. If an induction course is then limited to matters that affect all employees, rather than dealing with the specifics of one occupation, it is possible (for induction purposes) to bring together starters for a variety of jobs. The new craftworker, the new clerk, the new storekeeper all share some common information needs about the organisation, its function and its employment rules and regulations, and they can all attend the same training programme for these particular induction elements. Mixing occupations together in this way may help, too, in creating cohesive and co-operative attitudes between different sectors of the workforce.

On this basis, all the new starters on a particular day, whatever their jobs, will be kept together for at least the initial part of the induction programme.

Some organisations mix not only different occupations but also widely different levels of staff, though this is, perhaps, a more debatable practice. It must depend on the style of the organisation. If the emphasis is very much on reducing status differences, then it is appropriate for the new manager or supervisor to attend the same induction course as the new clerk or factory worker. If the view is that the authority and standing of senior staff should be reinforced, then separate induction is indicated. The actual content of an induction programme may also influence this point. For example, mixing a large number of staff from various levels for a film about company operations overseas may be entirely satisfactory. To do the same thing for a session explaining and discussing disciplinary and grievance procedures would be inappropriate if different procedures apply to different categories of employees.

In the large organisation a variety of approaches can be developed. All new employees may come together for some very general background about the company as a whole. Multi-occupational groups may share sessions on common employment practices, whereas smaller groups may be more appropriate for more detailed induction, specific to particular types of work.

Scheduling the course

The timing and length of an induction course will be influenced by decisions about who attends and about its content. There are, though, some general points to be considered that influence the final design of the course.

The danger of attempting too much too soon applies to all types of employees. A course with no practical job training that concentrates entirely on information about the company, its procedures and conditions of service may require up to five days if each topic is dealt with in detail. It would be most unwise, however, to devote the whole of the first week at work to such a concentrated and indigestible menu. This type of course is best phased over a much longer period perhaps one day a week for five weeks, or 10 half-days over a longer period.

The inclusion of practical job instruction in an initial training period enables the pure induction element to be similarly phased. For example, the induction element in the training programme for new recruits to a fire brigade is usually spread over the whole initial 12 weeks off-the-job training period. Highly active and practical job instruction on fire-fighting is interspersed with lecture-room sessions about the fire service, its history and traditions, and about more mundane matters such as conditions of service. The induction material is not all packed into the first week.

There are two categories of employee that are sometimes overlooked when planning an induction course: part-time staff and home-based or teleworkers. Yet effective induction is just as important for these staff as for full-time and work-based staff. Consideration needs to be given either to scheduling normal induction sessions at times within part-timers' normal working hours, or arranging extra sessions specifically for part-time starters. In any event, there may be some matters specific to part-timers (such as explaining how pro rata benefits are calculated and whether overtime is paid). These need to be included in part-timers' induction material, and may be sufficiently extensive to merit the production of a special leaflet for issue only to part-time starters.

There are always special factors relating to home-based workers. Some aspects of induction – such as general information about the organisation – can be covered by requiring home-based staff to attend relevant general sessions on the standard induction course. But these staff also need explanations of other matters specific to this type of employment (see Chapter 7 for details), which may indicate the need for special induction sessions. It is helpful for home-based staff to attend the organisation's premises for induction purposes, because this contributes to the development of a sense of organisational identity.

It is important to consider induction as a process that, though most obviously concerned with the first few days at work, extends over the much longer period between the employee's starting work and eventually becoming fully integrated and competent. Induction courses should be seen as no more than the formalisation of those elements of induction best met by systematic training. It follows that formal course attendance is best spread over a significant time period. The actual timing of each part of a course should be linked to an analysis of what information a new employee needs at various stages of the total induction process.

First-day induction courses should therefore concentrate on the immediate practical issues needed to cope with life at work, whereas later modules can reflect and encourage the expanding interest of the new employee, first in the work of his or her immediate section or department, then the wider setting of the company and the industry. This implies that some induction training sessions may best be scheduled for some months after the first day at work. For example, consider new professional staff (accountants, lawyers, engineers, etc) in a large multifunctional organisation such as a company conglomerate or a large local authority. It is not immediately necessary for them to study the very wide or complex organisational setting in which the particular functions or subsidiary companies are located. Their first few weeks are likely to be fully occupied in adapting to their own specific work situations and departments. But after, say, three months, it may be timely to organise an induction module in which they can learn about, and discuss, the broader environment in which their immediate work functions are based.

Reference

This book does not attempt to describe the related subject of job training or the skills involved in instructing new employees in technical skills. For a general text on planning and managing all types of training programmes, see R HARRISON, *Training and Development*, London, IPM, 1988.

7

The Induction Course:
Techniques and Content

It is inevitable that much induction training consists of imparting information, and rather less of developing specific working skills. Skills training may, of course, be a dominant feature in the first few weeks of employment for jobs in which recruits have little or no experience of the work concerned. The training of new fire-fighters at fire brigade training centres has already been quoted as an example. Similar emphasis on job training occurs in many factories where new workers have to be trained not in general skilled trades such as fitting, welding or bricklaying but in machine operation or assembly techniques specific to the particular plant. Operator training of this kind lies outside the scope of this book, except to note that a good deal of induction training can be integrated with formal job training, and to suggest that some lessons can be learnt from skills training about the use of appropriate training techniques.

Induction training techniques

Much work has been done in developing different training techniques appropriate to various forms of job or skills training. Reliance on chalk and talk or 'sitting by Nellie' has given way to a whole range of more relevant techniques, including discussion sessions, project work, and self-teaching methods through interactive computer systems. Sometimes less thought is given to techniques for induction training, where 'giving a talk to the new starters' is the only method used. Nothing is more likely to result in a rapid loss of trainees' attention than a succession of talks. The following type of programme is a recipe for boredom, frustration and a singular lack of success in securing an effective intake of information by the trainees:

9.30 am   Introductory talk by factory manager

43

9.45 am	History of the company: talk by personnel manager
10.00 am	Conditions of employment: talk by assistant personnel manager
10.45 am	Talk on sports and welfare: company welfare officer
11.30 am	Safety in the factory: talk by safety officer

The use of a range of training methods creates the variety necessary to maintain the trainees' attention and involvement.

Different topics demand different training techniques. Films, videos, slide-tape packages, wall-charts, overhead projector slides and other forms of visual aid will reinforce verbal forms of information and provide a more illustrative alternative to the straight talk. Every opportunity should also be taken of leaving the lecture room to see, rather than be told about, some aspect of the organisation and its work. Why lecture about safety when a guided visit to the factory, plus some practical demonstrations, will make a far more vivid impact on the new recruits? Where the purpose of a session is to influence emloyees' attitudes (say, towards their role in a local authority *vis-à-vis* the general public), group discussions will be far more effective than lectures. Issues of this kind require new employees to think things through for themselves, if on a guided basis.

The lecture room is a very artificial environment, and listening to lectures is an activity remote from the realities of working life. Training methods take trainees out into the working environment, and which require their effort and involvement, are far more likely to serve the fundamental purpose of induction – easing the process of adaptation to actual work.

Check-list of techniques

A check-list of techniques other than talks illustrates the wide range of training methods to be considered when designing an induction course.

Films and videos: particularly to show aspects of an organisation's work not readily accessible for new recruits to visit; and as a medium for communication by an otherwise remote top management in very large organisations. Videos produced initially for publicity and job training purposes can often be used in an induction course. In-house videos can be used to introduce top management; or to illustrate specific safety points.

Interactive video (IV), CD-ROM and CD-Interactive (CD-I): the rapid development of a variety of computer-based or computer-linked information and training techniques has widened the opportunities for self-learning considerably. Off-the-shelf programs are steadily coming onto the market to provide learning resources in many aspects of management and employment, and some organisations may have the expertise in their IT sections to produce tailor-made material for induction purposes. There is also an increasing use of employee learning centres equipped with PCs, video players and a library of learning packages, with open access to employees at breaks and after normal working hours. New employees should be introduced to such facilities and encouraged to make full use of them. Starters – who may be more aware of their need for information and training than some existing employees – are likely to be very receptive to such encouragement, provided they are given a practical demonstration of what is available, and how and when to use it.

Tape/slide packages: cheaper to produce than films and therefore more readily adaptable for specific induction purposes. Useful for explaining subjects that require a number of charts or diagrams. Can also be produced centrally in a large organisation and sent out for use by line managers.

Overhead projection transparencies: similar uses as slides, though supplementary to a conventional talk. Should be used to reinforce key points, and for fairly simple diagrams or charts. A typical example would be their use in a description of company organisation structure.

Visits: guided visits to explain a factory operation or production sequence. These are an essential element in induction for which films are a second best (the latter should be used only if actual visits are impracticable). A walk-through of any large building complex, pointing out the location of car parks, entrances, enquiry desks, canteen, rest and first-aid rooms etc is also useful, though may need supplementing with a map.

Hand-outs: a variety of printed material should be used to supplement explanatory sessions and provide a more permanent *aide-mémoire* for the trainees. Employee handbooks can be talked through when explaining conditions of service and employment procedures. Some printed publicity material may reinforce videos or visits. The company's annual report may provide useful explanatory and illustrative matter. Some companies produce employees' versions of their annual reports. Safety leaflets are also helpful.

Discussion groups: used much less generally for induction than in supervisory training, but a useful way of stimulating new recruits' interest in the organisation's policies and objectives. For example, instead of merely telling new retail assistants of the firm's procedure for dealing with returned goods, a training session can start with the question: 'Why do you think we exchange returned goods without query?'

Projects and self-learning: the discussion approach points towards discovery learning and methods through which new recruits have to find out information for themselves. Used particularly for A-level school-leavers and graduates, this may consist of giving a small group of new starters a couple of weeks to research a question such as 'What are the company's marketing strategies, and how and why have these changed over the past five years?' Other groups may be given different aspects of the organisation to study. All the groups are then brought together for a day, and each presents its finding to a group of senior managers who comment on and, if necessary, correct the information obtained.

Deciding the content

The actual subject matter of an induction course will be heavily influenced by such factors as:

● Are the trainees new to the industry as well as to the particular organisation? If so, then the course needs to include background information about the general economic or social setting.

- Are the trainees all destined for the same occupation? If so, induction training may be merged with normal job instruction. If not, the course will paint only a general picture of the working environment, leaving the detail either to a supplementary course specific to each job, or to normal on-the-job induction.
- To what extent is useful induction material readily available (eg publicity films, job training packages, information packs) from other sources? It is always worth researching the availability of suitable material from employers' associations, professional institutes, government sources (Central Office of Information). What material, too, is available within the organisation? Annual reports, employee handbooks, safety codes, advertising or publicity leaflets – all can be put to use in an induction course.
- What is the volume of recruitment? Are induction courses required frequently or only occasionally? If frequently, they can be fairly comprehensive; if only occasionally, perhaps by grouping together once a quarter all the new starters for the past three months, much practical initial induction will have to be left to line management.
- To what extent are line managers to be involved in the course? The danger of a course of any length run exclusively by personnel and training officers has already been referred to. If it is difficult for practical reasons to obtain line managers' involvement in the course (eg to talk about marketing policies or to take part in a discussion about contacts with the public) then there is a case for restricting formal course content, and emphasising systematic induction by line management within departments.

Check-list of content

The precise content of each course must therefore be tailored to fit the circumstances of the particular organisation. As a check-list, however, the content is likely to need to include information about some or most of the following:

Domestic information
  geography of the site
  cloakrooms and lavatories
  canteen facilities

rest and first-aid rooms
car parking, travelling arrangements
time recording

Health and Safety
fire exits and fire drills
basic safety rules, no-smoking zones etc
accident procedures
protective clothing
occupational health service
security alerts

Wages
wage and salary systems (including performance-related pay)
bonus schemes, including employee shareholding, etc
savings schemes
allowances (shift, overtime, standby, etc)
sick pay
deductions
explanation of pay slip
actual pay-out procedure

Other conditions of service
hours of work, flexitime, rest breaks
annual leave, absence from work, extra-statutory holidays
pension scheme and life insurance
car and other expense claims
disciplinary procedures
grievance procedures
general rules and regulations

Working matters
use of telephones, faxes, photocopiers
workplace security procedures
internal mail, including electronic mail
use of pagers
use of company transport
data protection procedures
equipment maintenance
energy conservation procedures

Welfare and other benefits
  sports and social facilities
  staff purchases
  suggestion scheme
  access to personal welfare counselling
  mortgage assistance, loans

Trade unions and employee involvement
  trade union membership or recognition policies
  who's who: shop stewards, safety representatives
  joint consultative systems: quality circles, briefing group system
  pay bargaining systems: national and local agreements

Employee development
  appraisal schemes
  training schemes
  assistance with professional studies, study leave, OU arrangements, etc
  promotion opportunity policy
  qualification incentives

Equal opportunities
  the organisation's policy standards of behaviour expected of employees
  rules regarding sexual and racial harassment

The organisation itself
  the organisation's mission statement and core values
  operational and other objectives and policies
  organisation structure, role of constituent companies, departments, functions
  managerial and supervisory hierarchy and who's who
  scale: numbers employed, annual turnover, capital and revenue budget, etc
  processes, production methods, functions
  public relations policies

The industry or sector
  nature and size of the industry or economic sector
  national/industrial organisations

relationship with government
relevant legislation affecting role, standards, functions, etc
place of particular organisation within whole industry or sector

Other items will need to be added to this list to meet the specific needs of particular categories of employees. One category that is growing in importance and needs special attention is the home-based employee or teleworker. In addition to a range of information common to all types of employees, home-based workers need specific information about:

- what equipment they will be given (eg computers, fax and modems) and what arrangements apply for its insurance and maintenance
- how they are to maintain contact with the office
- how, and from whom, their work will be allocated
- whom they should contact with queries about work or about their pay and other benefits
- how they are to deliver or transmit their work, and when or in what circumstances they are to call at the office
- what they should do if they are unable to work because of sickness or domestic problems
- what form of records they should keep about their work
- how they will be paid.

Individual industries or sectors will also have their own unique characteristics which require explanation. Chapter 9 goes into this aspect in more detail.

References

For another useful checklist of subjects to be included in an induction programme, see ACAS, *Induction of New Employees*, ACAS Advisory Booklet No. 7, London, ACAS, 1989.

8

Counselling and Probation

The whole process of becoming acclimatised to a new job may take several months. Induction does not stop after the first day, nor should the planned element of induction be limited to attendance at an induction course.

There is a need to make regular checks on the progress of new employees (ie induction follow-up) and to take action to put right any aspect that is giving the employee or the employer cause for concern. The extent to which such follow-up is formalised varies. At one extreme, it may consist of no more than the occasional informal chat initiated by the supervisor. At the other extreme, it is a documented series of appraisal interviews with each new employee, with written reports being passed from supervisor to personnel officer, all set in the context of a formally specified probationary period.

Which method is right depends on the type of employee, the general employment ethos or style of the organisation, the existence or otherwise of more general employee appraisal or counselling systems and, to some extent, convention and tradition. Certainly, the formal probationary period is more common in the public than the private sector, and this may reflect a generally greater emphasis on formality and documentation (not to say bureaucracy) in public-sector organisations.

Whatever method of follow-up is used, the principle remains that success in induction is enhanced by new employees' progress being closely monitored, and by corrective assistance being provided to deal with any problems.

It is also important to ensure that induction and probation procedures conform to the requirements of employment legislation, particularly if dismissal for unsuitability or misconduct has to be considered. The first two years of employment are the only period during which the employer can take such action without the risk of being taken to an industrial tribunal. This should not be taken as an invitation to treat new employees less fairly than established staff. It does emphasise, however, the need to make a thorough assessment of each new employee's suitability, and to be consistent and systematic both in helping new employees to succeed and in terminating their employment if all reasonable efforts to achieve such success fail.

Progress checks

The period during which induction follow-up is advisable varies with the nature of the job. A fairly short period of, say, less than three months may be sufficient where the following factors apply:

- The work is simple, with no significant learning problems.
- Employees on this work form a major and stable occupational group within the organisation.
- The general pace and flow of work is steady and not subject to frequent fluctuations of pressure or overtime.
- Existing employees have developed a welcoming and support- ive attitude towards new recruits.

Much longer periods may be necessary in other circum- stances, particularly where at least some of the following condi- tions exist:

- The work is complex and difficult to learn.
- The work involves much subjective judgement, based on an acute understanding of, and 'feel' for, the internal attitudes or politics of the organisation.
- The job is outside the main established routines of the organi- sation.
- There are large and unpredictable variations in workload or sudden and significant overtime requirements interspersed with slack periods.
- Existing employees have developed an unusually closed or introverted culture which is perceived by newcomers to be unwelcoming or even hostile.

Underlying the general principle of follow-up is the simpler view, often expressed by busy supervisors and hard-pressed personnel officers, that it is vital to weed out unsatisfactory employees at an early stage after recruitment. This is certainly a significant aspect of induction, though it should not set the tone for induction follow-up. New employees are unlikely to respond with enthusiasm to a management attitude dominated by thoughts of possible dismissal. To learn a new job quickly and well, and to adjust to the general mores of a new organisation, the recruit requires support and assistance, not threats.

One element of follow-up is entirely informal: the day-to-day interest shown in the problems and progress of new employees by their supervisors and managers. Supervisory training courses should include a session about this, though the general approach is one that applies to the management of all employees, whatever their length of service. The new employee, however, will respond particularly well to the friendly but perceptive enquiry: 'Any problems, George? What about that installation procedure that was bugging you yesterday? Show me how it's going now.' Note some subtleties about this apparently very informal enquiry:

- personal recognition: the use of a forename; the employee is an individual being treated individually
- a reference to yesterday, showing that the supervisor remembers things of concern to the employee; another example of individual recognition
- a positive check on a specific aspect of the job, not just a very general enquiry which can too easily be answered by a possibly inaccurate 'All right, thanks'
- a request to the employee actually to demonstrate the particular work item involved, not merely to reply verbally.

The supervisor should also keep an eye open for difficulties other than those related directly to the work. Symptoms of such difficulties may include late attendances, frequent short-term sickness absence, having to leave during the day because of the actual or alleged onset of such conditions as migraine or severe back-ache, fierce flashes of temper over very minor issues, a silent or withdrawn manner, or a marked failure to fit in with the social life of the working group. There can be a variety of reasons for these kinds of behaviour, and it is the supervisor's job to get to the bottom of any real problems and try to put things right. Typical underlying difficulties are:

- personality clashes with fellow employees, particularly those influential in the informal working group
- disappointment with the job for a variety of reasons, such as it proving less interesting or generating lower earnings than expected
- worries about ability to cope if not with the current work tasks then with what the employee perceives as the future demands of the job
- domestic problems, such as travel time proving longer than expected, or overtime requirements generating difficulties at home
- personal dislike of the supervisor – a particularly difficult matter if the feeling is mutual.

This last point illustrates the value of a follow-up procedure that involves other managers additional to the immediate supervisor. Progress or appraisal interviews with the personnel manager or the supervisor's manager after, say, one and three or six months' service permit confidential discussion of such problems as dislike of the supervisor or domestic crises. Occasionally it may have to be faced that a serious personality mismatch has arisen between employee and supervisor, and that consideration may need to be given to a transfer, if this is practicable. From a range of these interviews in different departments a personnel manager will also gain a useful insight into the differing abilities of individual supervisors in their staff management, and identify some who may need more training in relevant aspects of employee management.

If line managers conduct these follow-up interviews, they may do so to a pattern determined by a progress report form, to be returned to the personnel department, designed to secure consistency of standards across the organisation.

Check-list of progress reviews

There are a number of points about a new employee's progress that should be reviewed at regular intervals. These include:

Work output or productivity   Is the new employee progressing steadily from producing little or no output on the first day to the productivity levels expected of an experienced worker? Manual operations such as semiskilled assembly work may be work-studied, with detailed output statistics produced for bonus and production planning purposes. In such circumstances it is possible to use output graphs for each new employee which compare progress with the average learning curve for all workers. Fast or slow learners, or those hitting a bad patch in the learning process, can then be readily identified.

Some office work such as typing, word processing and computer inputting can be similarly measured. In other jobs a more subjective assessment may be needed.

Work quality   A fast rate of progress in terms of output is not always consistent with an absence of errors. What standard is the new employee reaching in qualitative terms? Does the rate of working need to be slowed down to improve quality? Is the new recruit taking so much trouble to avoid even the most minor mistakes that output is suffering? As with output, quantified data about error rates are very useful when making such assessments, though with much administrative and professional work statistical measurement is not possible.

Attitudes   What sort of attitude is the new employee displaying towards the job? Keen, interested and responsible? Worried, apathetic or antagonistic? And if attitudes are negative, what are the apparent reasons? Is there any evidence of a serious mismatch between the employee's ability or aptitudes and the demands and characteristics of the job? Is the employee adjusting to the organisational culture?

Relationships   How is the new employee fitting into the work group? What is the quality of the supervisor–employee relationship? Are there any personality problems, or problems of communication or compatibility? And, as with all these questions, what corrective action might be taken (by the employee, the supervisor or the personnel officer)?

Competencies   What specific competencies are needed in the job (ie a competency profile) and to what extent is the new employee demonstrating his or her ability to match this profile? Are there gaps which indicate specific training needs?

Attendance What is the employee's attendance record for sickness, other absences and lateness? If this is poor, are there any indications of the reasons?

Potential Is the new employee showing any potential for more advanced or different work, or for eventual supervisory or managerial work? It may be too early to consider transfers or promotion during the first few weeks or months of employment, but the indications of potential may well become evident at a very early stage and are worth noting during these early progress reviews for later follow-up. (See Chapter 9 for further comment on promotions and transfers). At some point after initial induction the new employee might be nominated to attend an assessment centre event to assist in the identification of promotion potential.

An important result of progress interviews should be positive action when this is required. The employee should know what is being done and why, and be told what standards or objectives are being set. For example, a decision may be made to transfer a not wholly satisfactory new employee from a very difficult factory assembly process to an easier type of work, with agreement between the supervisor and personnel manager that success on this easier work must be evident within four weeks or the employee's contract will be terminated. It is not unknown for such decisions to be effected with no clear explanation to the employee, who is thus unaware of failure on the difficult work or the risk of dismissal if this occurs on the work to which he or she is transferred. This is appallingly bad employment practice. The supervisor, perhaps with the personnel manager, should explain the decision and its reasons to the employee, set out what is now required in work performance, and encourage and assist the employee to make every effort to succeed. The four-week deadline for a final decision about continued employment must be made crystal clear and, preferably, supported in writing (an essential where formal probation extends into the period when the employee has a right of access to an industrial tribunal for unfair dismissal).

Lying behind many of the detailed points outlined above is a more general question: to what extent has the new employee adapted to the culture of the organisation and been accepted by colleagues and managers as a member of the team – as 'one of us'? Many of the factors influencing this are informal and are concerned with the behaviour and language of the management and workforce both in and outside work. Typical sources of difficulty for the new employee are:

- not being interested in social or sports activities which are major topics of interest and activity among the existing workforce
- for women who join a largely male workplace, the psychological discomfort of working in a 'macho' environment
- dislike of the type and amount of bad language used by managers and colleagues – or the opposite situation in which a new employee fails to understand and respect the higher (or different) standards of acceptability within the organisation
- an inability to socialise after work because of domestic responsiblities

Issues of these kinds are particularly significant if the organisation is widening its traditional range of recruiting to include categories of employees (eg women, ethnic minorities and the disabled) who have hitherto been largely unrepresented in the workforce. It is important in these circumstances to accept that what may need to be changed is the culture of the organisation rather than the attitude of the new employees. Equal opportunity issues lie at the heart of many problems of this kind, with a formal policy of broadening the constitution of the workforce being severely prejudiced by early leaving, caused by a refusal or reluctance on the part of existing employees to accept new and different colleagues. The emphasis in induction is normally on helping the new employee adapt to the organisation. But in circumstances of the type just described it is the organisation that needs to adapt in order to ensure the successful intake of new and different types of employees.

For the new employee, help with the general process of adjustment to the style and behavioural norms of the organisation can be obtained from an experienced and sympathetic mentor. This aspect of adaptation is not suitable for formal, course-based training. It is essentially personal to each recruit, so one-to-one advice and counselling is required. This may well be accepted more readily from a colleague than from someone who is perceived as senior in formal, hierarchical terms.

The legal aspects of probation

The inclusion of a formal probationary period in a new employee's contract of employment has significant legal implications. On the one hand, it may make it easier for the employer to dismiss an unsatisfactory recruit; on the other, there is an obligation on the employer properly to supervise an employee's progress during the probationary period.

A key case that helped to establish these principles was Post Office v. Mughal[1]. The precise circumstances of this case are of less importance than the statement by the Employment Appeal Tribunal (EAT) about the questions to be answered when a probationer is dismissed:

> Has the employer shown that he took reasonable steps to maintain appraisal of the probationer during the period of probation, giving guidance by advice or warning when such is likely to be useful or fair; and that an appropriate officer made an honest effort to determine whether the probationer came up to the required standard, having informed himself of the appraisals made by supervising officers and any other facts recorded about the probationer?

Note the emphasis in this statement on *appraisal*, on *guidance* (advice or warning), and on the final decision as to whether or not the employee has reached a necessary standard being taken on the basis of the appraisal *reports*.

The EAT went on to say that if these steps are taken by the employer, then a dismissal will be fair provided only that the employer makes a reasonable decision about the probationer's suitability. Further, the EAT expressed approval of six principles explained by the Post Office as governing their probation procedure:

1 Management must set the standards of capacity and efficiency required of probationers if employment is to be confirmed. This inevitably involves management exercising an element of subjective judgement.

2 The employer recruits probationers on trial and must decide whether new recruits measure up to the standards set.

3 During a trial period probationers are under continuous assessment and appraisal in a way that ordinary employees are not.

4 As probationers are on trial, and know it, their failures may be strictly judged, because they should be reasonably regarded as trying to do their best.

5 In ordinary employment it may not be easy for employers to satisfy an industrial tribunal that they have fairly dismissed an employee who comes up to average in capacity and performance. But a probationer is liable to be dismissed if the employer can satisfy a tribunal that the probationer did not come up to the standard laid down for new recruits to the established (ie non-probationary) staff. If an ordinary employee has been below standard but, after warning, improves, it is likely to be unfair to dismiss for the inefficiency or misconduct that occurred before the warning. But in the case of a probationer the employer is entitled to look at performance over the whole of the probationary period, and improved performance at the end of the period may not outweigh reasonable doubts about capacity or personality that are founded on the earlier period.

In general, the EAT took the view that although employers must make appraisals of probationers and take appropriate corrective action by way of advice or warnings, probationers themselves must accept that because they are on trial their performance may reasonably be judged against higher standards than those of non-probationers.

There are numerous other dismissal cases on record which confirm these principles. In Cusack v. London Borough of Camden[2] and Gray v. Grenvil Associates[3], probationers' dismissals were held to be unfair because of inadequate supervision and counselling, and an absence of warnings.

In two other cases, O'Kelly v. Royal Liver Friendly Society[4] and Schofield v. Ray Alan Manshops[5], findings of unfair dismissals were influenced by a lack of training during the probationary periods.

Because the service limit for eligibility to take a claim of unfair dismissal to an industrial tribunal was extended from 12 months to two years, there have been very few probationary cases at EAT or Appeal Court levels. However, the earlier cases described in this chapter still stand and their relevance is not limited purely to legal considerations. Taken together, the approach they put forward as to how probationary periods should be managed is one that can be commended as good personnel management practice, regardless of precise legal rights.

These cases point to the value of telling probationers to whom they should go with problems and ensuring that these persons, chargehands or supervisors understand their responsibility of helping newcomers to succeed.

The letter of appointment might usefully be quite specific on this point:

> During your probation, X has been specifically assigned to help you if you have any problems with your work. He/she is there to assist you and it is important that you take full advantage to ensure that you gain the greatest value from your probation period. If you are in doubt, ask – do not guess.

One other important point is clear from contract law: employees who are treated by employers as 'on probation' must be told very clearly of this employment status. 'Probation' may be used loosely as a general phrase to describe an initial settling-in period. However, if the employer wishes to benefit from the ability to apply the strict standards set out in the Mughal case, it is essential that probationary status is clearly specified in the contract of employment.

How long should a probationary period be? Some employers have assumed that because a dismissed employee has access to an industrial tribunal after two years' service, a probationary period should not exceed two years. That is not the case and there is no obvious legal limit to the length of probation. It is nevertheless good employment practice for the probation period to be kept to a reasonable minimum. If probation is taken seriously (and there is no point in using probation unless this is so) it must be recognised as a period during which new employees have a very serious uncertainty hanging over them. Will their employment be confirmed? It would be poor personnel management to maintain this period of uncertainty longer than absolutely necessary. The actual period, then, has to be related to the nature of the job and to a realistic assessment of the time taken for an acceptable recruit to reach an acceptable standard. In some simple jobs this might be as short as a month; in more complex work, six months to a year may not be unreasonable.

Regardless of the precise length of probation, or indeed of whether a formal probationary period exists at all, it is essential that all new employees are assessed for suitability before the risk can arise of a tribunal action for unfair dismissal. A failure to consider long-term suitability at this critical point can lead to serious difficulties if the unsatisfactory employee is allowed to continue after the first two years.

Access to an industrial tribunal begins after two years' service. In considering dismissals, it must be noted that if a notice period extends beyond this two-year point, then the right of tribunal access is obtained, even though notice was given before the two years expired. It is the date of the last day in employment that establishes the length of service, not the date on which a dismissal notice was issued. The only way of avoiding this trap, should a decision about dismissal be delayed until very close to the two-year point, is to dismiss summarily (ie without notice) and pay money in lieu of notice. It is essential that any dismissal letter is explicit about the date of the last day in employment.

However, in any effective induction programme, no such decision would be left so late.

Probation documents

Three forms of documentation are needed to ensure that all the requirements of probation are met:

1 A statement in the letter of appointment or in the terms and conditions of employment, specifying the probationary status and its duration.
2 At the very least, one document (report or managerial memo)

that provides evidence of an assessment of suitability for permanent employment. If the outcome of probation is dismissal, documented evidence of appraisals and of attempts at corrective action such as advice, training and warnings is highly desirable.

3 Written notification to the employee stating the outcome of this assessment. This might be confirmation of the satisfactory completion of probation, dismissal, or extension of probation.

A typical statement in the letter of appointment would be:

This appointment is on a probationary basis for an initial period of six months, though this period may be extended if it is decided that more time is needed to assess your suitability for normal/permanent/established employment.

(The exact phraseology for non-probationary employment varies. Public-sector organisations often distinguish between probationary and 'established' status.)

The wording must indicate that employment will continue beyond the probationary period if all goes well. Without any such reference (direct or implied) the employee might argue that the job is for a fixed-term contract, thus acquiring security of employment for the whole of the probationary period.[6] The appointment letter should therefore also indicate that employment may be terminated during, as well as at the end of, the probationary period. For example: 'Your employment may be terminated at any time during the probationary period if you are considered for any reason to be unsuitable for continued employment.'

The form of documented assessment depends on the appraisal and reporting systems in use. It may consist of the completion by the supervisor or manager of a standard appraisal form, designed and issued by the personnel department. It may be a standard report, completed by the personnel manager after discussions with the employee and the supervisor. It may be a less structured document, such as a memo from the supervisor to the personnel department, although in any large organisation a standard format is desirable to ensure consistency of approach across all departments.

It may also be part of the letter to the employee, giving formal notification of the outcome of probation.

This latter approach is acceptable where probation has been completed satisfactorily. A letter may then say:

I am pleased to tell you that you have completed your probationary period satisfactorily, and I can therefore confirm your continued employment on a normal/established/permanent basis from – (*date*) . . .

Extending a probationary period

A common practice of notifying probationers of the outcome of probation only if a dismissal or extension of probation is decided is to be deprecated. The employee who is told nothing at the end of probation may well be uncertain as to whether this indicates the beginning of normal employment, or dissatisfaction with his or her performance. In one case on record (Walker *v*. Wooley)[7] it was held that the absence of confirmation should have been treated by the employee as a form of warning. It seems highly desirable to avoid misunderstanding and worry, which can be done with a positive statement in all circumstances.

If progress has not been entirely satisfactory, the letter will need to make more specific reference to the results of assessment. Thus, for example:

Your initial period of probationary service is due to end on (*date*).

You will know from our recent discussion, however, that I am not yet wholly satisfied about your suitability for continued normal employment. In particular, I need to see a sustained improvement in the following aspects of your work: (*give details of shortcomings and reminders of advice and warnings*)

I have therefore decided that the period of probationary service should be extended until (*date*). If you maintain a satisfactory standard during this period, your continued employment will then be confirmed, and I hope very much that this will be the outcome. If, however, you fail to achieve and maintain the required standards I must now place on record that your employment will be terminated.

63

A follow-up discussion at this stage is also essential if employer and employee are going to work together to secure success.

For how long might a probationary period continue to be extended? There are no absolute rules about this: it is a matter of reasonableness and common sense. It is obviously undesirable to put off almost indefinitely the important decision as to whether or not a new employee is suitable. It is also questionable practice to extend unilaterally a probationary period if no mention of extensions has been made in the formal conditions of employment. As a very rough rule of thumb, one extension of between a quarter and half the length of the initial period seems a reasonable limit in other than very unusual cases.

Extending a probationary period beyond two years will not, of course, evade the two-year trap of the employee's right of access to an industrial tribunal. That right will accrue regardless of the status of employment. If, however, the probationary period has been unambiguously extended for clearly explained reasons, as in the example given above, an eventual dismissal for failure to improve within the terms of the letter extending probation is almost certain to be supported at a tribunal, provided that clear evidence is given of the employee's shortcomings and of reasonable efforts by the employer to correct them.

References

1 EAT 243/76 and IRLR 5th May, 1977
2 COIT 917/195, 1979
3 COIT 831/171, 1978
4 COIT 882/212, 1979
5 COIT 818/90, 1978
6 Dalgleish v. Kew House Farms (1982) IRLR 251
7 COIT 337/210, 1975
For a description of appraisal interviewing applicable to progress reviews, see T. GILLEN, *The Appraisal Discussion*, London, IPD, 1995.

———————————— 9 ————————————

Needs of Particular Groups

Most of the previous chapters have dealt with induction principles and procedures common to all new employees, from school-
leavers taking up basic manual or clerical work to newly
recruited managers. It has been stressed, however, that the design
of particular induction schemes should take into account the
specific characteristics of different types of work. This chapter
examines some of the different induction needs of some particular occupational groups.

School-leavers and young trainees

School-leavers have one unique characteristic: their lack of experience of paid employment. With adult recruits, even those
starting jobs different from anything they have previously undertaken, the employer can assume their general experience of the
disciplines of employment. But the employer who offers a
school-leaver his or her first job should recognise a responsibility
to assist the young person make a successful entry to the world
of work, as well as coping with the particular job.

Induction for school-leavers, consequently, merits more thorough attention than for any other group. Five broad areas of
learning and adaptation are involved:

- adjustment to working in a defined job role, in a structured
  environment, within prescribed rules and procedures
- understanding the general industrial, commercial or other setting in which the employing organisation is based
- understanding the nature and functions of the employing organisation itself
- learning the actual job
- learning to work safely.

Whereas these principles are of obvious importance for the school-leaver who is taking up normal employment, not all employers recognise and address the similar needs of young people on various government training schemes. But just because the trainee is attached only temporarily to the organisation and is not an employee does not reduce the need for effective induction. Inadequate safety training, for example, has led in some cases to the inexcusable result of a higher incidence of accidents among young trainees than among the main workforce.

In addition to the normal induction material outlined in the previous chapter, other elements to build into a programme for school-leavers and young trainees include:

- an early assessment of each individual's capabilities and training needs, because some may require more assistance than others to learn the job and adapt to the working culture
- planned and closely supervised work experience, with a particular emphasis on working safely and on the safety of others
- training in core competencies relevant to most jobs, eg communication skills, problem-solving methods, computer literacy, and job-related numeracy
- systematic reviews of progress, linked to coaching and counselling
- encouragement and support for embarking on relevant courses of study leading to nationally recognised qualifications.

National Vocational Qualifications (NVQs) are particularly useful in this connection, with their balance of a knowledge input with the development of practical job competence. The direct connection between theory and practice is of particular value to the non-academic young person who is unenthusiastic about beginning a more formal course of study.

There is a more general and longer-term approach to the preparation of young people for the world of work. Working together, schools and employers can provide insights by a variety of means into industrial and commercial employment during the latter part of pupils' full-time education.

Visits to local employers have been organised by some schools for many years, though if too large a visiting group is given no more than a standard tour of the factory the learning effect may well be very limited. Much more planning and co-ordination is needed by school and employer to make such visits worthwhile. Before the visit, scene-setting sessions in school can relate the activity of the company to elements in the curriculum pupils can be given check-lists of things to look for and ask about on their visit; afterwards, company managers can be asked to participate in group discussions at the plant and back at the school.

A much more powerful learning experience is 'shadowing', when a pupil spends a day (or longer) with a manager, sitting in on meetings and other activities, and observing directly what is involved in the particular job being shadowed. The CBI and some local Chambers of Commerce have given enthusiastic support to such schemes, but there is no reason any organisation should not make direct contact with a local school to offer a shadowing facility. The CBI emphasis has been on top management shadow-ing as a way of improving the image of industrial management as a career. A case can be made, however, for a much wider use of the method for a variety of types of jobs.

None of these pre-employment activities is a direct part of induction, but the organisation that opens its doors to pupils, in whatever way it and its local schools agree, will be making a general contribution to easing the transition from school to work. However, it will also have made its own induction task easier for those school-leavers it recruits locally who have already gained some understanding of the working environment they are about to enter.

Graduates

The graduate entrant with no previous working experience has very similar induction needs to those of the school-leaver. Grad-uates do not require quite such a basic approach: they are older, and their university experience should have gone some way to developing their self-confidence and self-teaching abilities. Many, of course, will also have had vacation employment, often in jobs that will have opened their eyes to the reality of life in the factory or office.

Partly because they are aiming for jobs on a career basis, partly because their academic experience will have generated (hopefully) an intellectually enquiring approach, graduates will need their induction to pay more attention than that of school-leavers to a study of the industrial and organisational setting in which their particular initial jobs are based. For example, a graduate joining a food processing company will want to know about the food industry generally (its scale, market and technical trends, export experience, etc), the role of the company within the industry, and the company's own sales, development, production, financial and organisational policies and objectives. A graduate entrant to a local government administrative post in, for example, a social services department will need to understand the nature of local government as a statutorily defined decision-making institution, how it obtains its resources, how it allocates resources between its various functions, and what the particular role of its social services department is within the total framework of a local authority.

Normal induction activities (short courses, planned work experience visits) can all be used. One other method, particularly suited to graduates, can exploit their academically developed ability to learn for themselves. This is to give graduates, either individually or in small groups, some form of investigatory project for which they have to find out for themselves much of the facts about their organisation and its setting. For example, a group of four or five graduate trainees in a large local authority might be given details of a small town suffering from traffic congestion. They would be asked to report back to a panel of managers on the steps that would be necessary to assess the pros and cons of alternative routes for a bypass. They would be expected to discover that a very wide range of council functions would be involved (engineering, legal, financial, environmental and political), while the task of presenting a complex issue by written report and verbal explanation is also excellent and relevant job training. In an industrial setting, projects might include such issues as the possible closure of a factory, the launching of an export drive, or the impact of robotics.

'Returners'

Many organisations now recognise the value of encouraging back into employment people who have been away from work for many years. In the main, these are women who left work to bring up their families, though some companies have also had success in recruiting men (as well as women) who have retired prematurely – perhaps co-incident with redundancy – but who are keen to return to paid employment, whether full- or part-time.

There are some special features of the induction needed for these re-entrants, some of whom may not have been in a job for as long as 20 years. The need for job training for those who are re-entering employment in work wholly different from that which they left is obvious. What is however not always given sufficient attention is the need for a considerable amount of updating training for those returning to the same types of work. It is all too easy for managers and those who have been in continuous employment to overlook the extent to which job methods and equipment have changed over the past decade. The most obvious example – and it affects all offices in all sectors – is the impact of information technology (IT).

Apprehension about the extensive use of computers is something that can deter the potential returner from going back to work or, if mishandled, can undermine the confidence of an older re-entrant. There is a commonly held myth among older people who have not lived through the office IT revolution that computerised systems are highly complicated, to be understood and operated only by young, agile minds. With today's user-friendly software this is, of course, nonsense – but saying so is not enough if returners are to be recruited and reintroduced to work successfully.

It needs to be made clear to potential returners that the new computerised world makes many jobs easier (and often more interesting) and that full training will be provided to help them adjust to the new methods of working. As to the training itself, it is very important that this is provided by someone with sensitivity to the older, inexperienced person's initial fears of inadequacy. There must be no talking down to the returner, but equally no prior knowledge should be taken for granted, and a patient, thorough, step-by-step approach is essential. In the first few days particular attention should be paid to terminology. 'Logging-on' is not thought of as jargon in the computerised office – but to the returner it may be incomprehensible. Everything new needs explanation.

IT developments are universal, but each organisation needs to identify for itself those other, particular elements of work that have changed since the returner last worked – and it is these that should be given priority in the induction process. There is another more subtle point: cultural change. For example, nurses who left the Health Service 20 years ago return today to find a different pattern or style of conduct, systems, and organisational structure and values. Changes towards a more informal culture have taken place in almost all organisations – typified by the widespread use of forenames regardless of hierarchical levels. Some returners find this difficult to accept, or mistake informality for lack of discipline or system. In the induction process this is something that may need to be openly discussed.

In all aspects of induction for the returner, one-to-one mentoring is to be preferred to the formal group induction course. Unlike young people, who are used to the group teaching situation, the older re-entrant may find that attending a course involves as much readjustment to an unusual experience as restarting work itself.

The managed career break

The previous section on returners made no reference to organisations that take specific steps to encourage their own staff who leave for domestic reasons to return when family responsibilities permit. Career break schemes are not usually thought of in an induction context, but they do constitute a planned, long-term approach to ensuring successful re-entry to work. Managed well, they should go a long way towards eliminating the difficulties touched on in the last section, and should reduce the amount of retraining and re-adjustment otherwise needed for the returner. Most career break schemes incorporate the following features:

- The employee who is leaving indicates formally a wish to return to employment within a specified number of years (often five after the birth in the case of maternity leavers), and accepts an obligation to participate in the updating arrangements made by the employer.
- In return, the employer guarantees a right of return (subject to unforeseen contingencies) to the same or similar work at the

same updated salary. The return may, however, be to a part-time or job-share appointment instead of on the original full-time basis.

- The employer arranges some form of updating experience and training during the career break. This may include occasional short spells of part-time work; attendances at short annual refresher training sessions (timed to suit domestic arrangements); and the provision of a home-based computer terminal or word-processor to undertake some home-working.
- Contact is also maintained by sending the employee house-journals, technical literature, company notices and reports or any other documentation that will help the employee to keep in touch with developments. There may also be the occasional home visit by the personnel or line manager, and the employee is also encouraged to 'drop into the office' from time to time on an informal basis, and is invited to company social events.
- A re-entry training programme is discussed and agreed shortly before the employee returns to work.

Although career break schemes have been introduced almost wholly for women leaving on maternity grounds, some schemes recognise that men may occasionally have to leave for domestic reasons (eg to look after an ageing or disabled relative) and that the same arrangements can then be helpful to both employer and employee. In all cases, the two purposes of managed career breaks are to avoid the loss of staff experience and to ease the transition back to work after lengthy absence. It is the latter that can usefully be seen as linked to an induction policy.

Part-timers

Some organisations operate excellent formal induction programmes – but only for full-time employees who can attend the day-long courses involved. Part-timers have always had the same induction needs as their full-time colleagues, but the growth in part-time employment which is so marked a feature of the current scheme emphasises the need to include part-timers fully in the induction process.

This is not only a matter of ensuring that part-timers are adequately informed and trained, it is also important attitudinally. Part-timers often feel that they are the Cinderellas of employment, overlooked for training and promotion and not told anything of interest about the organisation. Yet securing their enthusiasm and commitment is just as important as it is for the full-timers.

The issue is largely logistical. Part-timers need exactly the same induction information and encouragement as full-timers, but this has to be arranged during their working time. There are some organisations that arrange induction sessions for part-timers outside their working hours, expecting these employees to make special personal arrangements to attend. Whereas in a few cases – and if the part-timers willingly agree – this may be acceptable, it cannot be recommended as general good practice. Full-timers are not expected to give up leisure time for induction training. To expect part-timers to commit non-working time to induction is solving part of the induction problem at the expense of the attitudinal point.

On a more detailed level, there are two subjects commonly misunderstood by part-timers about their conditions of employment. Both subjects need clarification, preferably at the recruitment stage:

• There is the question of holiday and sick pay entitlements. Companies often describe these as 'pro rata to full-time provisions'. But what does this mean? Does a half-timer get two weeks' holiday instead of four, or four weeks' holiday at half full-time pay? Normally the latter – but this needs to be made clear.

• Overtime can also cause problems. Are overtime premiums to be paid for hours worked after a part-timer completes his or her standard schedule? Or is overtime payable only after a full-time week has been worked? The latter applies in a number of organisations, and although this may not be seen by part-timers as fair, if it is the company's policy it should be explained at the beginning of employment – not after a part-timer has put in some extra hours in the expectation of receiving time-and-a-half.

• Largely as a result of EU legislation and rulings of the European Court of Justice, many organisations have had to revise and improve part-timers' terms and conditions. In general, the legal position is that part-timers are now entitled to precisely the same rights and benefits as full-time employees – adjusted by appropriate pro rata formulae. The equalisation of pension rights is perhaps the most important example. Changes of this kind are not extensively understood by new part-time staff, and the implications (including invitations to join the organisation's pension scheme) need to be included in part-timers' induction programmes.

Job-sharers

Employees recruited as job-sharers have many of the same induction needs as all other recruits – particularly part-timers. There are, though, some particular characteristics of job-sharing that require additional consideration. These stem from the essential difference between part-time work and job-sharing – a difference about which some employers still seem confused. In a job-share two people share the responsibility for fulfilling the requirements of what would otherwise be one full-time appointment. The confusion arises when an employer describes as a job-share a situation in which the duties of a full-time post are divided between two separate part-time posts, each with its own and different job description. In a real job-share the sharers have a joint responsibility for the whole job; who does what as a matter of normal routine is a matter for them to decide between themselves, and each must be ready to undertake any part of the job. Three aspects of this arrangement require attention from an induction viewpoint:

- Any employee recruited to a job-share who has no previous job-sharing experience needs the requirements involved to be most carefully explained. Serious difficulties can arise if the obligation to get the whole job done is not spelt out, with particular reference to the company's expectations during holiday and sickness absence.
- The sharers' individual responsibility or involvement in finding or selecting partners needs to be clarified. Initially, job-shares are often concluded with a pair of applicants who have, as it were, found each other. What happens if one leaves? Will the

remaining sharer be expected to find a replacement or be allowed a veto on the company's selection? These points need to be thought through, discussed and agreed at the time of recruitment – not when a sudden crisis arises.

- The method of salary payment and entitlements to other benefits needs to be clear from the start. Is an arbitrary equal split of a full-time salary to be made? Is it going to be left to the sharers to divide a single salary between themselves? Are timesheets to be kept to assist in salary allocation? How are holiday and sick pay entitlements to be calculated if the sharers work unequal hours? Points of this kind can cause many problems if they have not been thought through and explained at the time of recruitment.

Homeworkers/teleworkers

Developments in information technology, combined with cost-saving considerations of office space, are resulting in steady growth in the employment of homeworkers. This is still a small-scale feature of the employment scene, but it is attracting interest and action, particularly for work which can be undertaken largely on an individual basis, assisted by personal computers linked by modems to the organisation's own computer network.

Many organisations' initial experiments with this type of homeworking involve existing staff who, for various reasons (mainly domestic), are interested in moving from office-based to home-based working. For these staff there are not the full, normal induction needs of newly recruited employees. It is a mistake, however, to consider that no induction of any kind is necessary. Experience has shown that staff who transfer to home-working can quickly feel isolated; they worry about becoming poorly informed about developments in their field of work and in what is going on more generally in their organisation. Three measures can help to reduce such alienation, and whereas all of these need to become standing features of home- or teleworking, their introduction and initial stages are very much in line with good induction practice:

- Homeworkers should be sent copies of all company documents – reports, notices, memos, journals – which they would have

74

received had they stayed office-based. Their managers should also send any additional material which on an office basis they might not normally have seen but which will help to keep them in touch. There might well be a monthly drill for this, with the manager sending a covering chatty letter about the work of the department. They should also be invited to company social events.

● 'Hot-desking' involves the establishment of an office location – it may not need to be more than a single desk – which a group of homeworkers can use when they call in to the office to collect or deliver work material. To avoid the feeling that they have been cut off from the office world, homeworkers need a territory there.

● The personnel department should be acutely aware of the possibility of homeworkers feeling isolated and out-of-touch, and should provide appropriate counselling. Homeworkers should be encouraged to 'drop in for a chat' with one of the personnel department's staff when they visit the office on a working basis, so that any such problems can be identified at an early stage.

The induction of homeworkers recruited externally poses bigger problems. They will have the same needs as the employees transferring from office to home, plus all the normal information requirements of all new recruits. Yet their domestic circumstances may prevent their attending conventional induction courses; and it is clearly difficult to provide the same type of relatively informal on-the-job induction by an experienced colleague which can be so effective for the office-based recruit.

There are no easy solutions to these practical problems. Short induction sessions may be a possibility – there are few homeworkers other than the severely disabled who cannot spend the occasional hour or so away from home. It may well be necessary for a job tutor to undertake initial training at the employee's home, particularly to check that the IT equipment and programs are operating effectively. Very careful attention certainly needs to be given to the quality of any self-teaching aids, with a 'hot line' available for new homeworkers to telephone for immediate assistance. Visits either to or from home to discuss progress and problems with the line and personnel managers are essential, particularly during the first few weeks or months.

Yet despite the practical difficulties of induction, the advantages of homeworking to employer and employee should in many cases far outweigh the cost of an initially heavy input of training and support.

Ethnic minorities

Recruits from ethnic minorities will be particularly sensitive to the personal and group attitudes of their fellow workers and supervisors, and to the general social culture of the workplace. Personnel managers and supervisors should be alert to problems which could arise, quite unintentionally, from the peculiarities of the organisation's formal and informal traditions and styles.

Particular attention needs to be paid, too, to any latent or actual friction between individuals. Some discussion may well be necessary between supervisor and existing employees, should actual or apparent racially biased attitudes put successful induction in jeopardy.

Apart from this general factor, language training can be a specific requirement in some circumstances, and training in the specific jargon and language of the trade is often desirable. Where large numbers of ethnic minority recruits are involved it is helpful to have recruitment and induction literature available in their own languages (eg Urdu) as well as in English.

On-the-job instruction and information should also be given by a speaker of the appropriate language if recruits' knowledge of English is limited.

How well recruits from ethnic minorities are integrated will depend to a significant degree on the extent to which the organisation has not only adopted an equal opportunity policy, but has taken practical steps to put this policy into effect. Such steps include action in the recruitment and selection field as well as in induction and training. Recruitment advertisements and the choice of advertising media can be used to show that job applications from ethnic minorities are welcomed, while the way such applicants are dealt with at all stages in the recruitment and selection process will be a practical demonstration of the validity (or otherwise) of any claim to be 'an equal opportunity employer'. More than one organisation that publicises such statements with every good intention has had its image severely dented when black applicants have been dealt with brusquely or rudely by front-line security or reception staff who have had no equal opportunity training.

Any effective equal opportunity policy will include provision for dealing with complaints of racial (and sexual) harassment. However extensive the equal opportunity training and publicity programmes may be, there remains the risk of individual cases of racial abuse or pressure. Any early experience of this by a newly recruited employee can result in the loss of a potentially valuable member of staff, or the beginning of an unhappy chapter of friction. Employees at large need to know that such behaviour will not be tolerated; ethnic minority recruits need to know how they should proceed should any such harassment occur.

People with disabilities

Equal opportunity policies and legislative developments are both leading to a more positive approach to the employment of people with disabilities. For induction purposes, it is important to recognise that there is no standard type of disability, and that the training needs of people with different disabilities vary considerably. All will need the same general induction assistance as other employees but consideration needs also to be given to different individual needs. Examples are:

- the use of hearing loops and braille keyboards for those with impaired hearing or sight
- wheelchair access to the workplace and to such facilities as the staff restaurant and lavatories
- safety arrangements, such as ensuring assistance with rapid escape in case of fire
- the use of any special aids and adaptations to equipment.

Many of these matters should be discussed with the new recruit before employment begins, and then explained and demonstrated when the employee starts work. To ensure effective induction it is often also necessary to provide guidance to supervisors and staff who may have prejudiced views about some forms of disability or

77

may be uncertain about how to help someone in a wheelchair or who has severely impaired sight, or about how best to communicate with the hard of hearing.

Managers

Because managers are usually recruited individually, and because their role often makes it difficult or inappropriate for them to be merged with more junior staff in a formal induction programme, their induction needs are often overlooked.

Yet the effectiveness of new managers can be achieved more quickly if at least some elements of their first few weeks are systematically planned. The main needs are usually:

- to get to know the formal and informal hierarchy of the organisation
- to meet not only their immediate seniors and juniors but also all the managers in other departments with whom their jobs involve contact
- to know the formal limits of their authority to make decisions without reference to higher or other levels
- to understand the informal expectations of other managers (and the trade unions) to be consulted before decisions are made, even when the formal rules appear to permit unilateral decision-making
- to discover the best sources of information and advice inside and outside the organisation
- to understand the nature and emphases in the organisation's external relations.

It is, consequently, very helpful for the manager to be given a carefully prepared reading package of relevant reports, key company memoranda, organisation charts, policy and procedure documents, the most important of the correspondence files, minutes of management meetings, and perhaps an annotated list of the main personalities with whom the job involves contact.

Cold print alone is not enough, and a programme of visits and discussions with relevant managers should be arranged for the first week or so. The personnel manager and the manager's own senior need to talk through and explain this programme with the new manager. The personnel manager has a particular role in these introductory discussions:

- to describe the informal style, methods, and groupings in the organisation, particularly where these differ from the formal structure and procedures
- to explain the key elements of the organisation's personnel policies and procedures as they impinge on the day-to-day work of the line manager.

During the manager's induction period it may also be helpful to arrange for him or her to sit in on various management meetings and on relevant joint consultative meetings with the trade unions, mainly to observe the organisation in action and to be introduced to colleagues and working contacts.

The new manager's senior should be particularly aware of the difficulty any newcomer has of adapting rapidly to the style and standards of an organisation, with the consequent risk that some of the manager's first decisions may be logically sound, but tactically unsatisfactory. Tactful initial assistance with more sensitive issues can often help to avoid the risk of the morale-shattering *faux pas*.

Industrial or occupational groups

Each industry, or other form of organisation or institution, has its own characteristics, problems or hazards which need to be explained to new recruits. It is not practicable to provide a comprehensive list, but examples are:

Agriculture: handling of toxic chemicals used in crop and pest control; safe tractor-driving methods.
Financial services: confidentiality of customer information; security systems.
Catering and food hygiene industries: personal and working hygiene.
Construction: hazards and safety rules for each site; procedures regarding disposal of scrap.

Health service: procedures and style of patient contacts; inter-functional relationship of administrative, nursing and medical staff.
Hotels: dealing with guests; guests' lost property procedures.
Local government: relations between officers and elected members; conduct regarding hospitality by suppliers.
Manufacturing industry: hazards specific to each trade, eg wood-working machinery in furniture trade; handling of radioactive isotopes; no-smoking zones, etc; product security regulations (ie searches of employee cars and bags).
Retailing: customer complaints procedures; staff purchasing regulations.
Gas, electricity, water: for outside staff, rules about production of identity cards to the public; for sales and service staff, customer relations and customer complaints procedures; personal ID arrangements for entering premises; safety regulations.
Information technology and computing: data security; access and password systems; back-up procedures.
The media and publishing: house style; libel and copyright legislation.
Education: the teacher-pupil-parent relationship; schools' rules and processes on discipline and truancy; extracurricular duties.

Personnel managers should, of course, produce their own comprehensive schedules of such key points specific to their particular sectors and organisations.

Transfers and promotions

If there is one group of employees whose induction needs are overlooked even more frequently than managers, it is an organisation's own staff who move to new jobs on transfer or promotion.

The degree of change involved in such a job change does, of course, vary considerably. At one extreme is the clerk who merely takes over a similar job in the same office. Here, there is no real need for induction, only for a systematic explanation of the requirements of the new job. But at the other extreme is the technician in a factory in Doncaster who is promoted to a head office technical sales job in London. In this case only the name of the employer and a few conditions of service such as the pension scheme remain unchanged. Otherwise, the degree of change is very much greater than it would be for a completely new employee who was already a London-based technical sales representative in the same industry and who joins the same sales office as the promotee. The new recruit already knows the industry, the type of job and the location. The promotee has to make all these adjustments at once, while also coping with the domestic upheaval of moving home. Personal counselling by the London personnel manager and on-the-job coaching by the technical sales manager can do much to ease this difficult transition.

Organisations with a sufficient inflow of new recruits to run formal induction courses on a regular basis would do well to consider transferred and promoted employees for attendance on at least parts of the courses. Existing employees will not take kindly to being treated as completely raw recruits. They will wish to be recognised as having already acquired valuable knowledge and experience of, for example, the industrial processes, the company organisation structure, and many of the employment rules and conditions. Selective attendance at those sessions of an induction course that cover new ground is therefore needed, and it is a sound approach for the personnel manager to discuss the course programme with transferees and agree with them which sessions will be useful.

Practical circumstances may make it difficult for them to flit in and out of particular sessions. The course may, for example, be held at a different location from their work base so that whole-day attendances or nothing are the only choice. In these cases the transferees' or promotees' knowledge of the organisation can be turned to good effect by arranging for them to assist the course organisers in running those sessions at which their attendance would otherwise be unnecessary.

Appraisal and continuous development

In many organisations a performance appraisal system can provide the vehicle for periodic assessments of new employee's progress. The trend is for appraisal to be part of a wider process of systematic performance management 'owned' and operated by line management, rather than being a personnel department procedure concerned solely with the identification of employees' individual training needs. Employee performance is assessed (and discussed with each employee) in relation to specified work targets or standards. Shortfalls in performance may indicate the need for further training or planned work experience; high standards of performance may suggest that the employee has talents that could be used even more effectively in different types or levels of work. New goals and action plans are agreed at each appraisal covering both work-based and personal development plans and targets.

Induction assessments can be built into the appraisal process and may be more effective when they are part of the whole performance management system. Whereas, for established employees, formal appraisals are usually held annually, one or two more can can be scheduled in each new employee's first year of service – say, at the three- and six-monthly points, with a final check on suitability for permanent employment shortly before the service entitlement for access to an industrial tribunal is reached.

It is essential that appraisals are not seen by line managers or employees as a one-way, fault-finding activity consisting solely of managers telling appraisees about their shortcomings. An effective appraisal is a constructive two-way discussion in which the appraisee is encouraged to raise questions or make comments and suggestions about any relevant matter – including things that the appraising manager might do to improve work standards or working relationships, or to provide a useful learning experience for the appraisee. It can be particularly valuable to managers to have comments from new employees about their perceptions of the organisation, thus bringing a fresh view to established working practices.

The inclusion of induction assessments within the general appraisal system is not a substitute for all the other elements of effective induction described in earlier chapters. What it does is help to integrate the management of new employees within the organisation's overall human resource strategies, and ensure that judgements about new employees' performance are related to the needs and culture of the organisation.

The whole of the induction process should also be considered as forming the first stage of each employee's continuous development – rather than as a discrete activity to be completed after a set period, separate from any wider employee training and development programme. The concept of continuous development is that all employees need to go on learning throughout the whole of their working lives. To quote from the IPD's members' guide to continuing professional development (CPD), the essential CPD principles include the following:

- Development should be continuous in the sense that the professional should always be actively seeking improved performance.
- Development should be owned and managed by the individual learner.
- Learning objectives should be clear and wherever possible should serve organisational or client needs as well as individual goals.

Although the IPD's policy is focused on professionals, the same general principles can be applied to all employees, and the time to begin inculcating this approach and encouraging employees to identify their own training needs and learning opportunities is clearly during induction. It means in practice that new employees are not just told what it is they have to learn in order to become fully operational. They are asked to suggest what they need to learn, and look for ways of doing so. Obviously, the new recruit will need much more assistance in this than the experienced employee. In particular, the new employee will have insufficient information about possible learning opportunities within the organisation. But a sense of personal involvement and responsibility for learning – rather than being the passive recipient of whatever training the management provides – can be fostered at a very early stage. At its simplest, it means that when a new employee encounters a problem at work, the supervisor says: 'What do you think you need to know to get over this problem?' instead of immediately solving the matter without explanation.

Continuous development implies, too, that the whole stage and content of formal training during the induction phase is compatible with the type of training that employees will encounter throughout their career. So if the emphasis in general training programmes is on learning through case and project work, that should be the style of induction training. Similarly, if extensive use is made of distance learning and self-teaching programmes throughout each employee's service, induction training should also make use of these methods. Again, the new recruit will need more personal help in the early stages, either by supervisory coaching or colleague mentoring, but if the emphasis within continuous development is on self-learning, this attitude (and the learning techniques to support it) must be built into the induction process.

References

1 INSTITUTE OF PERSONNEL AND DEVELOPMENT, *Continuing Professional Development*, London, IPD, 1995.

10

The Role of the
Personnel Department

This book has described a wide range of induction activities involving personnel officers, line managers and supervisors. In job training, and in helping the new employee adjust to life at the workplace, managers and supervisors play a most important role. Personnel managers cannot achieve effective induction by themselves: it requires a joint approach by the personnel and line departments.

It is nevertheless useful to identify the specific role of the personnel manager as well as four main elements of induction work that should be undertaken by the personnel department:

- the design of induction policies and procedures
- the implementation of particular aspects of the induction process
- monitoring the operation of the organisation's induction practices
- providing a welfare and counselling service for new employees to help them overcome induction problems.

Designing policies and procedures

The evolution of an effective induction policy is very much part of the personnel managers' general responsibility for developing effective employment practices. This policy should embrace the whole range of induction activities, from pre-employment procedures, through initial induction training to later follow-up and to the final decision about new employees' suitability.

The objectives of an induction policy are to assist new employees to adapt rapidly to their jobs, to help them become effective in their work as quickly as possible in order to reduce initial learning costs, and to create an enthusiastic, co-operative and adaptable workforce. Ultimately, as with all personnel policies, the objective is maximum organisational efficiency so that the company can improve its business competitiveness, or (as in the public sector) so that the organisation can provide the most efficient and cost-effective service.

Implementing an induction policy requires the co-operation of all managers and supervisors, and involves the commitment of time and resources. An induction policy, although initiated by the personnel manager, therefore needs to be discussed with and agreed by top management. Any initial reluctance to take induction seriously can be countered by the personnel manager demonstrating the costs and other adverse effects of a high level of early leaving; or of low morale, slow learning and poor performance among new starters.

An important aspect of induction policy is to ensure a consistent approach throughout all the stages of induction, and to obtain compatibility between the style and function of the organisation and the impressions and information the induction process generates in the new employee.

Consistency means that if selection and recruitment procedures are highly structured, then later stages of induction should be similarly structured. Sudden changes of style or pace between different stages of induction can be most disconcerting and do not achieve the steady progression from apprehensive raw recruit to confident, experienced worker which well-planned induction can produce.

The need for compatibility between the general style of the induction process and the character of the organisation has been mentioned in earlier chapters. It bears re-emphasis here. There is no point in the personnel manager designing a highly formalised set of induction procedures if the whole style of the organisation is one of relaxed informality. That type of organisation requires a relaxed, systematic but informal induction process.

Examples of induction policies

An induction policy needs first to consider these very general points about the character or style of the procedures that will best fit the nature of the organisation. More specifically, it should specify the key elements or requirements of the system. It might specify, for example, that:

- within the selection process, all short-listed candidates will be interviewed by their potential section supervisor and be given a short tour of their prospective workplace
- all selected applicants will be issued with a copy of the company handbook and of relevant sales or information literature about the organisation with the formal offer of employment
- all departments will produce a check-list of induction action to be taken on the first and subsequent days of work, with responsibility for various aspects of induction allocated to named members of staff
- all managers, supervisors and other staff involved in the induction process will attend relevant training courses
- all new employees will be issued with a Welcome Pack and attend a three-day off-the-job induction course within their first three months of employment
- the progress of each new employee will be reviewed and reported after one, three and six months
- a positive decision to continue or discontinue employment will be made for every new employee before the completion of 12 or 24 months' service.

This is not an exhaustive list: it illustrates the type of action it is helpful to specify in an induction policy in order to obtain systematic and consistent treatment of new employees, and to secure line management commitment and involvement.

Personnel department's own tasks

The precise allocation of responsibility for different parts of the whole induction process to the personnel department or to line management will obviously vary. Organisations with a large number of small subsidiary establishments (shops, area offices, small factories) are likely to depend more on line managers than large, centralised organisations in which the personnel department may handle most of induction except for on-the-job training.

It is unusual, however, for the personnel department not to be directly responsible for most, if not all, the following functions:

- designing and drafting most of the pre-employment documents,

ie application forms, contract of employment documents, employee handbooks, information leaflets, standard letters giving first-day instructions and the like
- conducting selection interviews in order to short-list applicants for final line-management decisions, notifying applicants of the results and issuing offers of employment
- informing line managers of the starting-dates of new employees
- meeting new starters, dealing with first-day documentation, and providing starters with at least some of their initial induction information
- planning and administering formal induction courses
- within these courses, running sessions that explain the conditions of service, company rules, welfare and social facilities, career development and appraisal schemes and other employment matters
- planning and co-ordinating progress checks on new employees and often conducting follow-up or counselling interviews with new starters
- planning and running training sessions on various aspects of induction to ensure that line managers, supervisors, and job trainers can perform their induction tasks effectively
- advising line managers on action to deal with unsatisfactory new employees and, if necessary, handling the administration of dismissal procedure.

Monitoring

It is one thing to have a set of defined policies and procedures. It is another to ensure that they are effectively operated and achieve the desired results. The personnel department should take an overview of the whole induction process in order to monitor its effectiveness and, if necessary, modify or develop the process.

Statistics

Early leaving is the major symptom of poor induction. The recording and analysis of labour turnover among new employees is therefore a most important part of the monitoring role. Statistically, this has several dimensions:

- the volume of early leaving (eg employees with under one year's service) as a proportion of all leavers. This analysis will show the extent to which total labour turnover of all employees consists of early leavers.
- the numbers and percentages of each month's or year's newly recruited employees who are still in employment at specified later dates. This form of stability analysis will show the incidence of turnover at different lengths of service.
- an analysis of the length of service of all leavers, which is perhaps the most useful statistic of all. At monthly or quarterly intervals this analysis might show the numbers and percentages of leavers with service of:

less than one week
one to 12 weeks
13–26 weeks
27–52 weeks
1–5 years
5–10 years
10–20 years
over 20 years

As with all statistics, these figures are of maximum value when kept consistently over a long period. A study of trends is often of more value than any one set of figures at a particular date.

To obtain the most value from statistics of the type just described, it may be helpful to produce them in three forms:

- by occupational category
- by department or section
- by sex and ethnic origin.

Analyses of occupational categories (eg craft, non-craft manual, general clerical, sales, technical, etc) may reveal significant differences which may highlight the need for improved induction for a whole occupational group across all departments.

Analyses of the early leaving patterns of each department may reveal significant differences for the same occupational group between different workplaces. One department, for example, may be achieving much more stability among its noncraft manuals than other similar departments. What is being done differently here? The answers may well result in improved induction across the whole organisation.

Analysis by sex and ethnic origin may reveal flaws in the practical application of the organisation's equal opportunity policy.

Other aspects

Not all monitoring can be effected through statistics. Some aspects will require the direct involvement of the personnel manager. These are likely to include:

- exit interviews with early leavers to probe the real reasons for such resignations. As well as solving individual problems, the personnel manager should look for patterns and trends. Is one particular supervisor perceived by new employees as unhelpful or antagonistic? Is there widespread disillusionment about earnings or job interest? Are some particular elements of one type of work generating serious learning or training problems?
- ensuring that departments are using their induction check-lists and are nominating the right employees for training in induction techniques. Do job trainers understand the learning problems of new recruits? Are new employees being shown the right things on their first day? Does the supervisor take progress checking seriously?
- reviewing the impact made on new employees of off-the-job induction training. Do the new starters understand the material used in these courses? Do the courses cover the points that may be worrying new employees? Do supervisors report any improvement in new starters' interest or understanding after attendance at these courses?
- studying the progress reports made by supervisors on new employees for problems and trends.

Welfare and counselling

It is particularly helpful to new employees to know that there is somewhere and someone they can go to with their worries or problems, and that they will receive a sympathetic and confidential hearing. This is not a matter of the personnel manager usurping the employee management role of the departmental head or section supervisor. Some of the points raised by new employees may well need to be put back into the line manager's court. The personnel manager must also encourage new starters to lose their sense of newness as quickly as possible and to stand on their own feet in their own sections. The new employee who runs to the personnel department with the slightest problem needs kindly but firmly to be directed back to the supervisor on all those points dealt with best at the workplace.

But there is a need for continuity of contact with a known person throughout the various stages of getting a new job and becoming acclimatised to a new organisation. The personnel officer who is met at the selection interview is the best placed to become this helpful and familiar face during the first few difficult weeks or months.

Furthermore, the new starter should be positively encouraged to seek an interview with the personnel officer if worries develop about things that the new starter may think it difficult to discuss with the supervisor. The supervisor may, of course, be the very problem that the new employee wants to talk about. Short-service employees who become discouraged and resign often do so over issues which, if discussed confidentially with the personnel officer, might well have been resolved.

Handling this confidential role is not easy. It requires a nice balance to be struck between regard for the new employee, the needs of the organisation, and the role and sensitivity of line managers and supervisors. The personnel manager must always bear in mind that the ultimate objective is the effectiveness and efficiency of the organisation, not the solving of welfare problems *per se*. But, of course, the exercise of judgement of this kind is the essence of much of the work of a personnel manager throughout the whole personnel function, of which induction forms only one (though an important) part.

Induction and Investors in People

The Investors in People (IIP) standard[1] provides a framework of principles about people management, which include a requirement for training at the point of recruitment and into which immediate and ongoing employee development policies and practices should be incorporated. The four principle elements of IIP are that:

- there should be commitment from top management to develop all employees to achieve business objectives
- the training and development needs of all employees should be regularly reviewed
- IIP employers take action to train and develop employees on recruitment and throughout their employment
- an IIP employer evaluates the investment in training and development to assess achievement and improve future effectiveness.

Running through the whole of the IIP approach is also the principle of linking organisational and training objectives, so that training plans and programmes derive from and support the organisation's business plans and objectives. All these principles apply to the various aspects of induction discussed in this book. Induction needs the support of top management. It should apply to all employees and be kept under regular review. Induction training should be thought of as a starting-point for training and development which continues throughout employment. Its effectiveness should be monitored (eg by assessing its effect on patterns of leaving), and it should be designed to relate to and support the organisation's values, standards, and business or service objectives.

Induction that is thus integrated with the organisation's overall aims and values, and that has a comprehensive and continuous training and development activity, can make a direct and valuable contribution to organisational success. Converting these principles into practice is a challenge for all managers, but the personnel manager can play a leading role in influencing managerial attitudes and initiating the necessary action plans.

References

1 *Investors in People and Management Standards*, published by the National Forum for Management Education and Development (the Management Charter Initiative – MCI) provides a useful summary of the IIP standard and shows how this links to the MCI's Management Standards.

Index